The Florida Man's Guide to Getting Divorced

Things Dads Don't Know About Divorce in Florida (But Should)

Vanessa Vasquez de Lara, Esq.

The Florida Man's Guide to Getting Divorced

Published in the United States of America

220201-02036.3.3

ISBN: 9781088148853

Here's What's Inside…

Introduction

By: Vanessa Vasquez de Lara, Esq.

<u>Your future self wants to say Thank You.</u>

If you've picked up this book and you're reading it, it means that you've either been thinking of getting a divorce, you're in the middle of a divorce, or you've survived a divorce and are back in court. I want to make sure that you know that your future self is going to appreciate having all of the information that we've put together for you in this book.

I've compiled some of the best professionals in the business to give you great advice that usually does not get discussed by anyone, even your divorce lawyer! Us divorce lawyers can only advise you on the issues that you bring to our attention, and many of the issues we're discussing here never come up.

You don't know what you don't know! And I, as your divorce attorney, don't know what YOU don't know!

I felt that there was a resource missing that could help divorcing dads understand what they needed to be aware of when they were in court. So, I reached out to some of the best experts to give the necessary advice on not only surviving your divorce but also *thriving* before, during, and after your divorce.

Before Going to Court

As a divorce attorney of almost 20 years, I'm always surprised by clients whose cases are made more complicated by the decisions that take place due to a lack of knowledge. It's always scary to ask the hard questions, so frequently, I get divorcing dads who heard or read something and ran with it. This is usually to their harm.

It is so important to be prepared for what's coming, even when you think that this will be a "simple" divorce. Preparation involves talking to an experienced family lawyer. You cannot line up your ducks if you have no ducks because your wife took them. You cannot make sure that you've covered all of your bases regarding your finances and your kids if those bases are hidden in your attic. You must face the reality of what is happening in your marriage in order to decide if you are going to fight for it or walk away from it.

Once you've made the decision to walk away from your marriage, you need to determine what your priorities are. As the saying goes, you can have everything but not at the same time. You cannot plan to get all of the kids' timesharing, all of your money from your marriage, and zero responsibilities for your ex. You will not get everything you seek. So, you need to decide what's your top priority so you can focus on getting what's most important to you in the divorce. Because unless you're made of money, you'll have to focus your resources on your top priority.

What to Expect

I always tell our clients, "You're not going to walk away with everything you want." From the beginning of their case, I encourage them to think about their priorities and rank what's most important to what's least important. It doesn't mean something is less valuable, but you must plan your battles based on your priorities. Suppose your priorities are a specific time-sharing schedule. In that case, we need to put our resources towards getting that done, potentially to the detriment of some of the other things you're trying to get. Perhaps we could do a specific division of assets or a specific amount of time for alimony payments. I try to ensure we are always realistic with our clients about what they can expect. We try to ask them, "In an ideal world, what will this look like?"

We follow that up with, "Okay, now that we know the best-case scenario, what would be your worst-case scenario? What's your order of priority so that we can try to make sure that we're focusing on what we need to focus on?"

By engaging an attorney at the beginning of the process, you come in with that information and education to realistically move forward through your case. The most difficult thing our clients will encounter is an unreasonable person on the other side who an unreasonable attorney backs. We try to make sure that we use our experience and depth of knowledge to give our clients a realistic portrayal of what they can expect in and out of court. Then we try to move the case forward with that plan or that map.

Consequences

Unfortunately, we see divorcing dads often in *the middle of a mess,* having already started or completed the divorce process, only to realize it's much more complicated than they imagined. They've missed many crucial steps along the way, which have caused the case to either drag out unnecessarily or led to bad results in court, which may be difficult to fix.

The most common mistake we see is when divorcing dads get a divorce without an attorney. Whether you've filled out forms provided by the courthouse or you simply haven't hired a attorney to assist you through this process, your rights are at stake! When divorcing dads don't have representation, **they don't know what they don't know**. They don't know the terms that need to be included, they don't know what pitfalls to avoid, and they don't know what to include to protect their kids and themselves in the future.

As a divorce attorney, I frequently have to pick up the pieces when you offer something unreasonable to the other side or when you offer something that is not in your best interest. This can include offering holiday schedules that are not in your child's best interest. Assuming that things will work out because you and the other parent are getting along *today* is not always the right decision. You have to make sure that the agreement in your divorce protects and benefits YOUR KIDS, as well as YOU.

You probably were getting along well with your ex when you resolved your divorce without attorneys. Unfortunately, a few months or a few years down the road, you're no longer getting along as well. Maybe there's a new partner on one side or the other. What ends up happening is that now you can't agree on everything missing from that marital settlement agreement and your parenting plan.

When something's not in the agreement and you can't agree, your only option is to go to court. I usually get contacted at that point because you've realized you've made a mistake and must go to court to fix it. You've realized that you need somebody to help you navigate what you didn't realize you were agreeing to and what you don't know.

The Most Common Problem

One of the most common things I will tell my clients concerning time sharing is that it's typically the issue that becomes the most contentious.

People are fiercely protective of their children. When they're not getting along, the biggest issues we see relate to their kids. Divorcing dads get a bad rap. Although, as a family, a couple may have decided on family roles, during the divorce, this becomes a point of disagreement. Although the parents may have agreed to the mom staying home or handling certain issues with the kids, during the divorce, those marital decisions and divisions of labor become a claim that the dad was not involved or did not handle any of the children's issues. This is not necessarily the case, but it is a regular argument in court.

Fathers are a necessary part of our children's youth. We need this generation's children to have involved dads. This is what our firm works so hard to achieve. We work to make sure that Fathers get to be in their children's lives because children without their fathers are more likely to have issues, including mental health, behavioral, and adjustment issues.

My Encouragement to You

I want to make sure that you get out of this book that there are many things you don't often consider when moving forward with a divorce. I've gathered an amazing panel of experts to provide information on topics people don't always realize are connected to divorce.

My goal is to have an educated divorce client, whether my client or another attorney's client. You should be educated about the different issues connected to a divorce that are not typically explained or thought of in the middle of a divorce or after you go back to court after your divorce because things are not working the way they should be working.

I hope you will be an educated divorcing or divorced dad who can better understand the process and all of the areas connected to the divorce so you can achieve your goals in the best way possible.

And I look forward to helping you when your family problems become legal problems because divorcing dads deserve to be a part of their children's lives.

Working for your best outcome…

Chapter One
Life Coaching After Divorce

By: Dr. Gisell Lopez

No one's life is perfect. We all go through tough times, make mistakes, and face unexpected challenges. Sometimes, though, things happen that are beyond our control, like divorce. If you're going through a divorce, you may feel lost, alone, and uncertain of the future. You may not even know what you are feeling.

It's important to remember that this is only a temporary setback. This, too, shall pass. I think we never lose. We always learn. Every experience in life teaches us a lesson to move on to what's next. We are continually evolving, and tough experiences and challenges in life are the stepping stones in the journey. You can get your life back on track and use this experience to improve yourself.

According to studies, the most commonly reported major contributors to divorce were lack of commitment, infidelity, and conflict/arguing. The most common "final straw" reasons were infidelity, domestic violence, and substance use. More participants blamed their partners than blamed themselves for the divorce. Since every person is different, it is only natural that different issues would surface for someone in a divorce situation. I can only discuss some common themes I have seen in my practice and what I support clients with as a Licensed Clinical Psychologist offering life coaching, therapy, and evaluation services.

First, I'd like to apply the quote from ancient Chinese philosopher Lao Tzu: "If you are depressed, you are living in the past. If you are anxious, you are living in the future. If you are at peace, you are living in the present."

One of the first things I support divorced clients with is the grief of losing the life that used to be. With that, feelings of sadness and frustration may come up. There are thoughts about, "What could have been? What could I have done differently?" I encourage my clients to allow themselves that grieving process and support them in moving through it. The only way out is through!

The second aspect is that divorce proceedings, especially when children are involved, can have ups and downs when going through the tunnel. This can be a difficult time in which support is essential. Going through the dark, scary, uncomfortable tunnel means you will eventually see the light.

The third thing many of my divorced clients experience is, "What now?" Once they reach that light, some hesitance or insecurity can come up. That would be the "future is anxiety" part of the quote. The main thing is to focus on the present moment because that is all we have. It is important to start dreaming about and planning a new vision for life after divorce. I work with clients on taking committed action toward the future vision, one day at a time.

Many of today's solutions for those seeking support after divorce involve trained professionals putting the client in a box and giving them an intervention, a checklist, that approach of "I am the expert." However, I firmly believe that YOU are the expert in your life. At times, untrained people with a focus on continued selling lead so many to feel hopeless and disconnected, going around in circles and not getting anywhere and not seeing results.

- Each person's circumstances are unique, so it is important to feel like someone is being with you and providing a space for you when seeking life-coaching services.

- Every step is tailored to you and the goals you have in mind.

- Through working together, you feel that you can achieve your goals.

- Seeing the possibility of healing and eliminating past obstacles.

- Hopefully discovering possibilities that you never imagined.

You must feel that your life coach is supporting you in thriving. Not only is it important to know their years of experience and training so that the professional serving you has the expertise you need and deserve. It is also important to know whether they are involved in ongoing continuing education to ensure the latest research informs their practice.

You want to work with someone who understands you and what you are going through, right?

- Maybe someone who knows the guilt that comes with seeking success in your own life while trying to remain connected to your family and friends.

- Going through their life challenges and understanding how times of change can feel lonely, hopeless, or frustrating.

- They're committed to their growth through self-development, continued education, and self-care to be a space for you and share experiencing amazing results in their own life.

When you work with a life coach, you are not working with a trained professional, but you should feel that you are with someone who creates a clear space where you can feel seen and understood. Someone who walks the walk is not trying to take you somewhere they haven't been.

What Is a Life Coach Anyway?

A life coach is a professional who helps people make progress in their lives. They help people have better relationships, careers and lives in general. The difference between life coaching and therapy is that life coaching focuses on setting and achieving goals, while therapy focuses on mental health and emotional healing. I provide both services in my practice, yet I will focus on life coaching after divorce for this chapter.

Seven main areas in life are important for all of us:

- Social & Family Relationships

- Career & Educational Aspirations

- Financial Security

- Physical health/leisure

- Life's routine responsibilities

- Society & contribution

- Mental, emotional, & inner well-being

Life coaching should focus on these areas and the misconception of balance. We are not octopuses. We cannot focus on all these things at once. The misconception of balance placed upon us, especially in our society, is that we have to have it all together. That is so unrealistic and honestly impossible! As humans, we have a specific affinity for attention and focus and a certain amount of energy reserves that can be put out.

In obtaining life coaching, focusing on one or two goals/priorities at a time is important to get the desired results.

How Are Results Achieved?

My preferred way is to use the manifestation formula (similar to Cognitive Behavioral Therapy concepts that are evidence-based best practices), which states beliefs, thoughts, feelings, and actions equal results.

When this formula is reverse engineered, which is a technical term meaning dismantling things to find out how they work, we go backward, exploring:

- What are our current results?

- What do we want the results to be?

- What are the current actions being taken?

- How do those actions need to change?

- What are the thoughts and feelings associated with the current actions?

- What core belief is associated with those thoughts and feelings learned in childhood or through difficult/important life experiences?

As the meaning-making machines we are as humans, we make everything up. We decide what our beliefs are, so if the beliefs which are the core of this formula are self-limiting beliefs, we can shift them and make a conscious choice to believe something different that serves us. That leads to desired thoughts and feelings and, in turn, causes us to take different actions and obtain different results.

We are the only ones who can provide the perspective through which we view our life. We create that lens. It's easier said than done, *but nothing changes if nothing changes.* Someone once said, "The meaning of insanity is doing the same thing repeatedly, expecting a different result."

In shifting what is on the inside, what is on the outside will shift. It is one of the laws of the universe, the law of attraction, which states, "As within, so without." Everything around us is a mirror of our internal reality. What we tell ourselves is a self-fulfilling prophecy. I believe it was Henry Ford who said something like, "Whether you believe you can do a thing or not, you are right." Clients ask me, "Does this life coaching thing work?" I'll reply, "What do you think? You will prove yourself right."

Anything you try will only take you part of the way. You are the one who gets to implement anything you learn or discover and continue on your journey to what you desire. I always give the example of someone who wants to lose weight. They go to a nutritionist who shares the diet and exercise regimen that will likely work for them based on their professional opinion. The person then goes home to continue eating poorly and not engaging in any physical activity and complains to the nutritionist that this is not working. Of course, the nutritionist can only take you part of the way. The rest is up to you. It is the same with life coaching.

After going through a divorce, wanting to better yourself is common. You may have been in a relationship for years and suddenly will find yourself single and alone. Maybe you were the one who wanted the divorce, or maybe it came as a complete shock. Regardless of the circumstances, divorce can be a very tough time. One of the best things you can do for yourself during this time is to get a life coach. A life coach can support you in navigating your way through this difficult time, decide what is next for you, and make sure you are on track.

A life coach can support you with accountability, being present, and how to shift your mindset. They will also help you determine if coaching is right for you and what you can expect to achieve from coaching.

Life coaching is a great way to help you get your life back on track if you are going through a divorce. Through coaching, you will be able to set goals and achieve them. You will also learn how to be independent and start dating again. If you have shared custody of your children, a life coach can help you devise a co-parenting plan that works for everyone.

Whatever your circumstances, life coaching after divorce can help you better yourself and manifest the life you want.

Here are examples of divorcing clients who have benefitted from life coaching.

Dating Dan

Dating Dan had been married to his wife for ten years when she came to him one day and said she wanted a divorce. Dating Dan was heartbroken. He had no idea things were so bad. His wife was always critical of him, and he started feeling like he couldn't do anything right.

After the divorce, Dating Dan decided it was time to start dating again, but he was nervous. He didn't want to get hurt again.

I gave Dating Dan an analogy to think about. Imagine performing in a comedy club where everyone in the audience hates knock-knock jokes, and that is your main style of comedy. People in the audience will probably not laugh, or they may criticize your style. Some people may even go as far as to leave the comedy club altogether. Now picture being in a room with knock-knock joke enthusiasts, truly die-hard fans of knock-knock jokes. The reaction will be completely different. You might get a standing ovation. People may even line up to get your autograph and picture with you. That is what it is like to be with the wrong person and then meet the right person.

He took things slowly, meeting new people online and attending low-pressure first dates. Eventually, Dating Dan met someone special. She laughed at his jokes and made him feel good about himself. They started dating seriously, and Dating Dan began to feel confident about not looking back.

Moving On Molly

Molly had been divorced for a few years. Her husband had cheated on her and was abusive. They had a daughter together, and Molly was determined to ensure the little girl had a good relationship with her father. Even though he wasn't allowed to take her to his place, Molly would have him come to her house to spend time together.

Several years passed, and Molly's ex-husband remarried. He also had another baby with his new wife. Molly still focused on his life instead of moving on with her own. She continued encouraging him to come over alone so they could spend time with their daughter.

She had dedicated her life to being a wife and mother. She didn't know how to move on. Molly decided to try life coaching to figure out what she wanted.

After a short while of working together, she started re-discovering herself. She took up new hobbies, spent time with friends, and began exploring her interests. Slowly but surely, Molly found herself again. She realized that she still had a lot to offer the world.

Your Story

Your story can be a success story by trying life coaching after divorce. That may sound ambitious, but the possibilities are endless. There is no limit as long as we believe in ourselves.

Here are some tips to consider for life after divorce:

1. Give yourself time to grieve.

Divorce is a major loss, so feeling sad, angry, or confused is normal. Allow yourself time to process these emotions. Cry if you need to, talk to a friend, and do whatever else you need to do to make yourself feel better.

2. Get rid of anything that reminds you of your ex.

This includes photos, gifts, and any other reminders of your marriage. It may seem painful initially, but creating a fresh start for yourself is important.

3. Focus on the positive.

It can be easy to dwell on the negative after a divorce but focus on your life's positive aspects instead. What are you grateful for? What do you enjoy doing? What are your goals and dreams?

Focusing on the good will help you move forward.

4. Manifest what you want.

Use the power of manifestation to attract what you want into your life. Visualize yourself surrounded by love and happiness, and believe you deserve it. The Universe will respond to your positive energy and help you create your desired life.

5. Take care of yourself.

During this time, it's important to take care of yourself both physically and emotionally. Eat healthy foods, exercise regularly, get plenty of rest, and find ways to relax and de-stress. When you take care of yourself, you'll be better equipped to handle whatever comes your way.

6. Seek support.

Contact friends, family, or a support group if you feel alone or lost after divorce. Talking to others who have been through similar experiences can be helpful. They can offer advice, comfort, and understanding.

7. Be patient with yourself.

Recovering from divorce takes time, so be patient with yourself. Allow yourself to heal at your own pace. There's no need to rush things. Take each day as it comes, and trust you will get through this.

No matter what challenges you're facing after divorce, remember that you are strong and capable of overcoming them. Use these tips to help you shift your mindset into getting your life back on track and creating the future you want.

Life coaching after divorce can be a great way to help you move on from your marriage and create a bright future for yourself. With the help of a life coach, you can discover your wants and needs, set goals, and manifest the life you desire.

Life coaches have the power to support you in making your dreams come true. We must be specific and clear about exactly what it is that we want for ourselves, our family, or our business because without this essential step in manifesting anything into reality, nothing will happen!

Today is the first day of the rest of your life, so make it count!

Chapter Two

Mental Health Services Aren't for the Weak; Mental Health Services Make You Stronger

By: Rebecca Amster Cantor, LMFT

Surfing the Breakup Tide

I live in Miami, which means I think about the ocean. Every day, I think about the ocean in some way. When the moon is full, I think about the extraordinary rise in high tide, which sometimes causes beachside communities to flood. When my kids have school projects for their environmental classes, I think about climate change and rising sea levels. At the beach, I think about the peace and tranquility of the endless song of the waves. In the wintertime, I think about our local endangered species, the manatee, and how humans need to take action to protect this native and vulnerable population of animals. When a hurricane comes, I think about the surfers riding the storm.

Going through a breakup can be intensely stressful for all family members. Most people experience the loss of an intimate relationship in much the same was as they experience the death of a family member. Their reactions are often similar.

In 1963, Dr. Elisabeth Kubler-Ross wrote her seminal book, *On Death and Dying*, in which she first postulated the five stages of grief, which have become widely accepted in the mental health community more generally as experiences of loss. The five stages are denial, anger, bargaining, depression, and acceptance. These experiences of loss can be quite overwhelming for some people in the wake of a break-up. Being awash in an overwhelming emotion is like losing your surfboard while trying to conquer a wave. You're suddenly overwhelmed with water, feeling like you're drowning, and desperately need to come up for air. Mental health services can be what you need at that moment. Therapists are beach lifeguards who help you return to the surface.

How to Know When It's Time to Ask for Help

When my client first walked into my office, she didn't understand why she was there. After all, Jodi*[1] was a mother of five children and had been an active and caring parent since the birth of her first child. She was a classroom volunteer and a committee member in the PTA and helped organize Teacher Appreciation Week every year. Her kids were all involved in extra-curricular activities, and Jodi got them all to their soccer practice, Tae Kwon Do, and choral rehearsals on time. The kids always had clean and neat clothing. They always had packed healthy lunches, right down to the carrot sticks. Jodi didn't understand why the judge wanted her to see me to help her cope with her divorce. Jodi was a model parent.

As I began our conversation, I asked Jodi about the stressors of raising five children and the logistical challenges she must face every day when school is dismissed. The children needed to be at their activities, never mind getting

---

[1] All clients' names have been changed to protect their identity.

dinner ready and doing all that laundry! Jodi
seemed at ease and relaxed, so I asked her about
her family support. Her parents had greatly
assisted the kids, but recently, they had
retreated and were unwilling to help as much.

However, Jodi told me with great enthusiasm
that she had met several other moms who were
very supportive and helpful and offered to
carpool whenever she wasn't feeling well
enough to get the kids to school on time. I asked
Jodi what she meant by "not feeling well
enough" to drive the kids to school. I thought
maybe Jodi had a comorbid illness that was a
source of stress and potentially debilitating in
some way. "No," Jodi said. "Some days, me
and the other moms get together and drink wine
and complain about our exes. Red wine seems
to go straight to my head, and I can't get up the
next day."

"Oh?" I asked, "About how often does this
happen?"

"Maybe two or three times a month."

"Are the kids often late to school on those
mornings?" I asked out loud, wondering if there

was a long history of tardiness that would negatively impact both Jodi's pending time-sharing case and her children's academic performances.

"Only by 20 or 30 minutes," Jodi answered dismissively.

By now, my "therapist" senses were on alert. I asked Jodi questions about whether she thought it was okay for her children to miss a significant portion of their school day several times a month. Jodi agreed that it wasn't great, but she also indicated she had no choice because she couldn't get out of bed on those mornings after she'd been drinking wine.

"Jodi," I asked, sensing that I was about to learn some impactful information, "even when you're not with the moms, do you still drink wine at home?"

"Sure," Jodi said, "After running around after five kids every day, I need a drink."

"Would you say you drink more or less when you're with the moms?"

"Oh, definitely, I drink more when I'm with the moms. When it's the kids and me, I drink two glasses of red with dinner, but with the moms, it could be twice that."

In other words, Jodi drank between 15 and 20 bottles of wine monthly. She was drinking daily to cope with the stress of "running around after five kids all day." Now, Jodi had been handed the stress of getting divorced.

Most people generally cope with stress in a way that doesn't impact their every day, overall function. Some strategies for coping with stress are quite helpful and healthy. For example, some people will make art, meditate, take long walks, or talk it out with friends to help them cope with internal stress. Some strategies, while still functional, may be less healthy. For instance, some people eat too much and gain weight; conversely, some eat too little and work out too hard. Some people will "trauma dump" on their friends and family, while others limit their communication and interactions.

There can come a moment when the less functional strategies become non-functional and when things you used to do to help you no longer work. Eating too much leads to health complications, distancing yourself from your friends leads to total isolation, or when your one glass of wine at night becomes the whole bottle every day, it is clear that it's time to seek mental health services.

In the context of a divorce, your lawyer will often ask you for information you don't know or don't know how to obtain. She will ask you questions that you don't even understand. (What does "shared parental" even mean?) Sometimes trying to answer those questions and juggle a new life separate from your partner with new routines for your children who aren't used to change is more than your current stress-coping strategies can handle.

No one is ever prepared to handle the fallout of the break-up of their family. It's a loss! You're grieving. Sometimes, from where you stand, you can't see that your strategies for handling stress have failed you. Here's an analogy you can use to determine how you're doing: When you feel as though you are in the middle of a hurricane, being pulled under by that ocean wave, for whatever reason, it's time to ask for help.

Alphabet Soup: The Difference Between LMHC, LMFT, Psy. D., Ph.D., and M.D.

All mental health providers are trained to help the mental health of our clients to the best of our abilities. How we are trained vastly differs from how we think about the best way to help our clients. While each of us is biased in thinking our method is the best, the truth is that no single approach to mental health services is the best or the right way. You need to find a good fit for yourself. If you think your therapist is helpful, you've found the one for you.

LMHC: Licensed Mental Health Counselor

A licensed mental health counselor has been trained to utilize various therapy techniques to help clients with mental health issues. After an assessment, an LMHC will design a treatment plan and goals tailored to your individual mental health needs. An LMHC is often a good choice if you're looking for specific one-on-one counseling to assist you in developing and strengthening your coping skills and individual resilience.

LMFT: Licensed Marriage and Family Therapist

Like an LMHC, an LMFT is a psychologist trained to use various mental health techniques to help you with mental health issues. An LMFT has received specific training around systems theory and developed an understanding of how different members of a couple or a family will behave in the context of their family. An LMFT is often a good choice in helping you work with your relationships, whether with your spouse, ex-spouse, children, or other close personal relationships.

Psy.D.: Doctor of Psychology

A Psy.D. is a clinician who brings a specialized skill set to the clinical setting. Often capable of administering various psychological evaluations, a Psy. D. may be the person you see who can diagnose you, your ex-partner, or even your child. Children often are referred to

Psy. D.s when there is a suspicion of ADHD, for instance.

A Psy.D. may conduct a social investigation when there is a question about where your child should live most of the time, diving into not only your individual psychological history but quite possibly the psychological and social history of your family of origin well. Psy.D.s are generally very helpful to the court and to the guardians ad litem, in making long-term recommendations regarding time-sharing and treatment goals for individual therapy. Psy.D.s are often talk-therapists in their own right.

Ph.D.: Doctor of Philosophy in Psychology

Rather than a clinician who treats patients, a Ph.D. is often an expert you may hire in your family law cases to testify for your case. Ph.D. s are interested in research and in doing and publishing the research around a wide range of clinical issues, whether that be about parental alienation, childhood trauma from divorcing parents, or the efficacy of different treatments for varying mental health disorders. You may find your contact with a Ph.D. somewhat limited, but your attorney may find their services as an expert witness invaluable. As a practicing clinician, I find the research conducted by Ph.D.s to be illuminating and instructive.

M.D.: Psychiatry

An M.D. in psychiatry is a psychiatrist. Colloquially known as "the guy with the drugs", psychiatrists are mental health professionals who went to medical school on their way to becoming mental health professionals. Psychiatrists have done all the basic medical school work, including rounds in all parts of a hospital dealing with all aspects of physical health that you would expect of any doctor. Psychiatrists then added more learning and training in psychiatry, often spending years in the psychiatric departments of hospitals. They are often skilled diagnosticians with years of experience around the more robust mental illnesses such as schizophrenia, bipolar disorder, and those mental health diagnoses with psychotic features. Psychiatrists do also prescribe psychotropic medications. They know about how they act on the brain, interact with other medications, and how to start and stop taking them over time.

It is important to note that there is no shame and no blame in taking psychotropic medications for however long you need them, even if you need them for the rest of your life. No brain is the same as anyone else's, and psychotropic medications can be lifesaving. If you were diabetic and needed insulin daily for the rest of your life, you would take it. You wouldn't wait for your pancreas to "figure out" how to make insulin. The same is true for psychotropic medications. If your doctor prescribes medication to improve your mental health, by all means, take it.

When the Court Appoints a Mental Health Professional

"In family court cases, no one ever wins, and the children always lose."

In my 20+ years as a family law practitioner, I have never seen a family case go through a fully litigated trial, and the children come out better for it.

The traditional court system was never designed for family cases. Consider this: in a traditional court case, one injured party sues the other, they argue for a bit, have a trial, and ultimately, one person pays the other person some money. Then the two parties never speak to each other again.

In a family law case, the questions the court must wrestle with aren't always, or even often, about financial issues. The questions are about what is in the children's best interests and how best to share custody or decision-making. After a trial, the two parties are expected to be able to speak to one another in a professional, courteous, and even friendly manner until their children reach the age of majority, and ideally even beyond.

How Can a Therapist Help Me in My Family Law Case?

A therapist can be an invaluable resource for your Family Law case. It's not hyperbole to state that we therapists can help you become a better parent.

Jose and Rosa litigated for years after the court finalized their divorce. While they were abiding by the terms of their time-sharing order with their two children, Carol and Alex, alternating weeks in their home, the two parents found themselves in court time and time again, filing motions for contempt for not sharing the responsibilities of decision-making for their children. When Jose filed a Motion for Contempt for Failure to Buy Blue Shirts for Minor Children's School Uniforms, the parents hadn't ever been in the same room except for hearings for over a year. The judge had seen enough and referred the parents to me for Parenting Coordination.

Walking the parents through their concerns about their children's well-being, I realized they both wanted their children not to suffer because of their divorce. They wanted their children to be anxiety-free, grow healthy, and develop normalized romantic relationships. I asked them if they thought they had protected Carol and Alex from their conflict, and they both said yes.

"Really?" I asked, looking up from my notepad.
"What color shirt is Alex wearing to school
today?"

Rosa and Jose erupted into a shouting match,
each accusing the other of manipulations,
bringing up the history of their 12-year
marriage, of every transgression, every hurt,
every insult, and vile hate they had for each
other. After 10 minutes of yelling and
screaming, they paused for breath.

I cleared my throat, and they both started and
looked at me. It was clear that they had
forgotten I was sitting there, witness to their
contempt, hate, and unresolved conflict. "If you
can forget I'm here, then I'm sure you can
forget the kids can hear every word you say
when you're on the phone with each other, too.
Your kids are witness to your conflict. You're
scaring them. Alex doesn't know what color
shirt to wear, and he wants you to approve of
him. How can he feel secure in your love and
approval when, every other week, you can't
even approve of his clothing?"

I worked with Rosa and Jose for a year, but at that moment, they realized their conflict would impact their children for a lifetime if they didn't find a way to manage it. After about six months, Rosa and Jose reported something like a miracle. They had attended a middle school band concert, sat together in the audience, and watched their daughter's face light up when she realized her parents were not only both in the same room but were seated next to each other so they could both beam with pride at their daughter's concert.

The Calm after the Storm

Therapy isn't always, or even often, a lifetime commitment. Most people who take advantage of the therapeutic process do so when they find themselves caught up in a hurricane of life circumstances, when they feel very much out of control and are drowning in their emotions. A good therapist will help guide you at that time in your life.

In therapy, you can gain insight and perspective into understanding your impulses and reactions to others. You can learn new and healthy coping skills for stress when your old anxiety-handling patterns are no longer working. You can find better ways of communicating with your exes so that you can move forward to co-parenting in peace. You can even find more effective ways of communicating with others, ways to set healthy and appropriate boundaries, and ways to self-care when your former partner repeatedly tries to hurt you in some way.

Therapy can be episodic as well. Many of my clients will see me weekly for several months, less frequently for several more months, and then we'll conclude therapy. It's not unusual for my clients to check in with me six months later for a "tune-up." Sometimes my clients face yet another set of life circumstances for which they will benefit from more frequent sessions until they develop and hone new skills to help them move forward.

After a hurricane lands in Miami, there is often a wake of devastation left behind. Trees are downed, the power is out, and homes are often damaged by wind, rain, and flooding. Food rots in refrigerators and freezers that no longer work. Not a single person would blame a homeowner for how their home looks after a category five hurricane barrels through.

The same is true for me as a therapist. I do not judge my clients or blame them for finding themselves in the chaotic wake of a storm. I only have one question: How can I help you?

Chapter Three
From We to Me:
Empower Your New Life by Up-Leveling Your Image

By: Lee Hayward

What if, by changing your clothes, you could create the opportunities you desire, such as a great first impression on a new friend, a dating profile picture that attracts the right person, and a judgment in your favor?

I'm Lee Heyward, and my job is to help clients up-level their lives by changing their clothes.

I have always loved fashion and had an innate sense of the power your image has. I didn't realize until working with countless clients and growing my business that having an authentic image is like having a magic wand.

Over the years of working with my clients, I've realized that the divorce transition provides an opportunity to rediscover and redefine your most authentic self. It's a moment when you decide who you want to be, how you want to feel, and what you want to look like as you build your new and improved future.

As you read that, you may think, "I already know who I am," but on the journey from we to me, you may find moments when you want to ramp up your confidence, remind yourself who you truly are, or make sure that you present yourself in the most strategic way to get the result you want in this new life. I hope this chapter will give you a framework to help you feel confident and in control in the moments that matter as you step into your new future.

The Power of Image

Your image is the outer portrayal of how you feel about yourself or your self-concept. Here is where the secret of the magic lies. An amazing image isn't about wearing designer clothes or looking perfect. It's about portraying yourself on the outside in complete alignment with who you authentically are on the inside. Your image matters because, whether you realize it or not, it drives every result you get in life.

If you're like most people, your image is something that happened to you, not something you strategically chose to get the results in life you want. Your parents probably told you what you could and couldn't wear as a kid. When you're older, you base your choices on what you like, but they're often tempered by the feedback of peers or an inner pull of what you think you *should* do. When you're married, your spouse weighs in on what they like or don't like and sometimes even buys your clothes for you. This creates a hodge-podge image that we think makes us who we are, but when examined closely, you realize it's often missing the key ingredients that make us who we truly are.

Whatever future you desire, you'll get there faster with an image that makes you look and feel fantastic. In this chapter, I'll show you how to do that.

What Is an Image

Let's back up a moment and look at what an image is. Your image is made up of an inner and outer image.

Your inner image is how *you* see yourself or your self-concept. This image drives every result you get in life, everywhere, all the time.

Your outer image supports how you see yourself. It comprises external factors that, combined, frame how *people* see you. These external factors combine what you wear, how you groom yourself, and your nonverbal communication.

These two image systems act as an operating system to help you feel confident in who you are and make others feel confident in you. When these two systems work together with clarity and purpose, magic happens. You gain a superpower that is unique to you. Opportunities start to show up. If one system is weak or confused, it can negate the efforts of the strong one.

For example, maybe your inner image helps you walk into court 1000% confident that a judge will side with you. But if your outer image tells the judge he can't be confident that you're the best choice, then your image operating systems are working against each other.

Interestingly, the way you dress has the power to strengthen both of your image operating systems. It has the power to give your self-concept a jolt of confidence and help others sit up and take notice of who you are, feeling confident in who you say you are.

Discovering the clothing or outer image items that make you feel like a superhero can create amazing opportunities in your life. It's this superpower that I like to call your mental edge.

The rest of this chapter will walk you through up-leveling your outer image. But as you do so, remember who you truly are so that you level up from a place of total authenticity and not what others have told you.

Your Mental Edge

When you wear clothing that makes you feel like you can conquer the world, you gain something you can only give yourself. It's unique to you. It's a mental edge over how you were even seconds before putting those clothes on.

Rhonda Rousey, one of the Ultimate Fighting Championship's highest-paid fighters, does her hair before every fight. Why is this remarkable? She has a team of people dedicated to helping her win. They are responsible for making sure that every possible thing she might need to think about or do is taken care of, including, theoretically, styling her hair. Her job is to rest, fuel her body, and go into the ring and win.

It turns out that a task as unremarkable as doing her hair is one of the most important ways she prepares to win a fight. She does it the same way every time. She always does it alone, and the action she says transforms her into her fighting mindset. When her fight hair is done, she has her mental edge. She knows she can win.

What do you need to create your mental edge? What must you do to walk into a room and feel confident and in control? How can you curate an outer image that makes a great first impression?

You Never Get a Second Chance to Make a First Impression

You've heard a thousand times how important it is to make a good first impression.

Let's start by talking about first impressions. Upon meeting someone for the first time, your impression of them is formed in seven seconds: 1… 2… 3… 4… 5… 6… 7. That's not a lot of time.

Typically, in seven seconds, you haven't even had an opportunity to open your mouth and speak. Research has shown that your impression of someone mostly comprises your appearance and nonverbal cues.

A Harvard study conducted by psychologists Nalini Ambady and Robert Rosenthal rated college professors based on one group of students' first impressions and then another group of students' impressions after having them as a professor for an entire semester. The first group only watched 10-second video clips of the professors with no sound to form their impressions. The second group took their class for an entire semester. The study showed that the first impression made from 10 seconds of silent video created almost the same impression gleaned from students who had an entire semester to form an opinion about the professor.

Thin Slicing

Ambady and Rosenthal's study created a term called "thin slicing." It means you make very quick inferences about the state, characteristics, or details of an individual or situation with minimal or thin slices of information. Judgments made by thin slicing are often as accurate and sometimes more accurate than judgments made over a long time.

Genetically, we are hard-wired to make quick decisions, everything from how much you feel you should trust someone to whether or not to buy a certain house. These decisions are made in a matter of seconds by unconscious thinking called rapid cognition.

Malcolm Gladwell wrote an entire book about this called *Blink*. It's all about the thinking that happens in the blink of an eye. His entire book was inspired by police officers stopping him because they thought he was someone else.

When Gladwell was asked about where the idea for *Blink* came from, he said this.

"Believe it or not, it's because I decided a few years ago to grow my hair long. If you look at the author's photo in my last book, *The Tipping Point*, you'll see that it used to be cut very short and conservatively. But, on a whim, I let it grow wild, as it had been when I was a teenager.

"Immediately, in very small but significant ways, my life changed. I started getting speeding tickets all the time, and I had never gotten any before. I started getting pulled out of airport security lines for special attention.

"One day, while walking along 14th Street in downtown Manhattan, a police van pulled up on the sidewalk, and three officers jumped out. They were looking, as it turned out, for a rapist, and the rapist, they said, looked a lot like me. They pulled out the sketch and the description. I looked at it and pointed out to them as nicely as possible that the rapist looked nothing like me. He was much taller, heavier, and about fifteen years younger (and, I added, in a largely futile attempt at humor, not nearly as good-looking.) All we had in common was a large head of curly hair. After twenty minutes, the officers finally agreed and let me go. On a scale of things, I realize this was a trivial misunderstanding.

"African Americans in the United States suffer indignities far worse than this all the time. But what struck me was how even more subtle and absurd the stereotyping was in my case. This wasn't about something obvious like skin color, age, height, or weight. It was about hair. Something about the first impression created by my hair derailed every other consideration in the hunt for the rapist. The impression formed in those first two seconds exerted a powerful hold over the officers' thinking over the next twenty minutes. That episode on the street got me thinking about the weird power of first impressions."

Just recently, I took my daughter to school and walked out at the same time as one of her classmates' fathers. I was wearing a bright blue dress. You couldn't miss me. I'd never talked to this gentleman before; he didn't know what I do for a living. We started a conversation, and by the time I reached my car, he had hired me to work with his wife and later himself. What if I had worn gym shorts like everyone else dropping their kid off at school? We would have said hello, but I doubt it would have converted to a sale. Instead, I was wearing a great dress. It made me unique. It made me stand out. It changed the first impression I presented. Ultimately, that dress created opportunity.

That's what a good first impression can do. It can lead to new relationships, new friends, and, most importantly, success in whatever you desire.

Achieve an EDGE

In my work over the years, I've developed a formula to help you create a mental edge and, even more importantly, keep it. This formula offers you an edge to finally define the future you truly want and how you want to show up in it. It's made up of four pieces, and it only works when you have every one of them in place.

The first piece comes from dressing in a way that intentionally engages the people you want in your life.

Next, it's important to dress as if you've already achieved the success or goal you're after. If you desire to land a job that will help you purchase your dream home for you and your children, you need to present yourself as if you've already landed the job, whether you have or not.

Then you have to keep it real. This means that everything you do must align with who you are. The fastest way to lose an edge is to pretend to be something you're not or to dress in a specific way because you think you *SHOULD*. Often, things that make you a little weird or quirky make people want to get to know you, so authenticity is key.

Lastly, you have to be consistent in the way you present yourself. Remember, people believe what they see, so if they see you on an off day, that's the impression they'll remember.

Consistency is the piece of the formula that helps you keep the edge you create.

Thinking through how you present yourself and using these four pieces creates an edge for your self-concept and the momentum of the future you want to build.

The EDGE formula is easy to remember:

Engage

Dress As If

Get Real

Every Day: Commit to Consistency

You're ready to get dressed. Now all you need to do is walk into Bloomingdale's and ask for the section where you'll find clothing to help engage people. They would look at you like you were crazy!

Rather than sending you to Bloomingdale's, let me reverse-engineer this for you so it is very simple to figure out how to create and maintain your edge.

Engage Others

Let's start by looking at how you can use what you wear to engage others, whether to stimulate conversation or a new relationship. First impressions are made before you've even had time to open your mouth. Engaging people is all about intentionally connecting with them in some way to gain their intrigue and trust. I say "intrigue" because, for someone to engage with you, they have to be intrigued by who you are. Otherwise, you're probably missing opportunities because people aren't motivated to talk to you.

One of the easiest ways to create engagement with others is to wear clothing that helps you stand out. The goal is to create an image that helps people know you exist, plain and simple. People can't get to know you if they don't even notice you. The idea behind getting dressed is to be noticed.

The idea is not to dress in a way that makes you STICK OUT. When you stick out, you're attracting the wrong attention. You want to dress in a way that makes you STAND OUT as someone who looks and feels put together and confident.

You may think that walking into a room and having all eyes shift to look at you sounds awful. That's not what we're talking about.

A few years ago, I worked with Stephanie. She is one of the most amazing people you'll ever meet. She's a caring, friendly, beautiful, and fun person. Before we met, people would invite her to a party, and she wouldn't go. She said she preferred to stay home than deal with the pressure of walking into a room without the safety net of having a spouse with her. Stephanie had divorced the year before and was rediscovering how to feel confident. I asked Stephanie what it would take for her to walk confidently into a party alone. She said she would need two things. The first was to look amazing, and the second was to make it so people would walk up and talk to her.

To achieve this goal, there were two main changes I helped her make to her wardrobe. For starters, I changed the fit of her clothes. By putting her in clothes that fit better (hers were a little too big), she instantly gained a sharpness about her that made you take note of her. It made her stand out. It intrigued people to learn more about her, so they would come up and want to speak with her.

While wearing slightly too big clothing, she inadvertently hid her entire self, not specific parts of her body. When you hide, consciously or not, people don't notice you. It takes a lot more effort to engage others you desire to be in your life when, at first glance, they don't notice you.

The second change was infusing authenticity into her wardrobe. Stephanie didn't feel amazing because she was wearing clothes that didn't make sense for who she truly was. She was wearing what she thought she "should" wear. She looked good and well-dressed, but there was no authenticity, so she never felt truly amazing. We readdressed what was possible for her from a clothing perspective and found pieces she had thought she could never wear, but when she put them on, she felt better than she ever had.

After working together, she sent me a note that she had met an amazing man, ironically, at a party. She said she got dressed and remembered feeling good about how effortless it was to look and feel amazing. She wasn't looking for love at this party, but because she looked and felt so confident, this gentleman couldn't help but notice her.

How can you stand out? What could help you intentionally connect and engage with more people in your life? What could you wear to feel amazing and make others notice you without saying a word?

Dress As If

Dress as if you've already achieved the result you're after. It sounds simple, but this is the piece of the EDGE formula most often overlooked. Rationally, it makes sense to think that you'll dress better and invest in yourself *after* life calms down or you get the job that helps you build your new future. The problem with that thinking is that you may never get there. Instead, when you act as if you've already gotten the result you want, you portray an image that helps you create the opportunities you desire.

I recently told a client looking to up-level her love life that if she wanted men to stop taking her to Applebee's, she needed to dress as if she always eats at the hottest new restaurant in town. We planned her up-leveled wardrobe as if she had weekly dates with the love of her life at the hottest restaurants in town. She has started experiencing new and fun places to eat both on her own and on dates.

What are the "As Ifs" that are most important as you design a new future you love?

Let's examine a few places you might need the Dress As If strategy on your divorce journey:

Court Appearance

In court, it's your job to appear as if the judge would be crazy not to side in your favor. What you wear in court is your way of speaking to the judge before you even have a moment to speak. How you dress can tell the judge that you have it all together, and they should be on your side.

This means you dress in a way that looks put together with every detail thought out. Your attorney can advise you on the style of clothing to wear for specific court appearances. However, the rule of thumb is to wear clothing that fits well, is wrinkle-free, and looks put together and professional for a court of law.

Remember, you dress to speak to the judge without saying a word.

Running into the Ex

Anytime you run into your ex, whether planned or not, you want to look like you are thriving and doing awesome without them. It's human nature. Therefore, even if you're not feeling awesome, use your clothing to boost your feelings. Wearing clothes that make you feel good will elevate your mood and appearance. Take the time before you leave the house to change into the clothing you have that puts a spring in your step.

Reentering the World of Dating

Get Real

Getting real with yourself is about embracing the most authentic version, from your unique personality to how your body is shaped.

Sometimes authenticity is the hardest thing for you to see for yourself. This is what I'm able to see within my clients. People always ask me if I walk around thinking, "Ugh, you should dress better." Sure, some things I see catch my eye, but I don't see people and judge them as a fashion mess. I do see certain people I meet or who pass me on the street whom I can tell have an impactful presence but haven't figured out how to authentically portray that on the outside.

You have a newfound confidence when you truly get real with yourself and dress authentically. It comes from embracing who you are, your unique personality, and knowing how to dress your body shape to feel good in your skin. You look in the mirror and see the lion version of yourself instead of a cat.

How you think about yourself shapes every decision you make and every result you get. It's your self-concept. You must be sure that the person you see yourself as is who you are.

Before clients work with me, I ask them to fill out a questionnaire. One of the most important questions on the entire thing is: **What makes you a little weird?**

My dad used to say, "Everybody's weird. Your perspective makes them more or less *weird* in your eyes." I've learned since that the things my teenage self called "weird" are the things that make others sit up and notice you. Your quirks, all the little things that make you weird, are the things that make you most authentic and more intriguing to potential clients.

Embracing your true self sounds easy, but for people who've dressed by the "rules," it can take some practice to find what feels and looks unique. You can invest any money on clothing, shoes, or even a new car, but you're wearing a costume if they don't feel authentic. You hide who you are when you wear clothing that feels more like a costume. When you dress authentically, you'll notice an extra skip in your step, stand taller, and feel prouder. That's the feeling you tap into. Never accept anything less than that feeling.

I recently had a client try on a jumpsuit that she would never have tried alone. I laughed out loud when she came out of the dressing room because she had morphed into a runway model strutting her stuff as she showed me the jumpsuit. For her, that article of clothing made her feel amazing, like a model, so it tapped into her true authenticity.

With men, I'm often shocked at how much taller they become when they walk out of a dressing room wearing clothes that are truly right for their personality. They stand taller and prouder without even realizing it, completely changing their presence.

The key is to be real with yourself. It's a much easier and more fun way to go through life!

Every Day: Commit to Consistency

This part of the EDGE formula requires a decision. No matter where or what you're doing, you're committed to presenting yourself in a certain way. This is how you'll maintain the edge you've created. When you maintain your edge, you're able to make an impact on those around you, inspire your children, and create opportunities around you.

It's about deciding that you will not only look and feel great when you walk into a big meeting but also when you walk into the gym. Instead of wearing the baggy gym shorts and a T-shirt with a hole you've had for years, you choose sportswear that continues to give you both a mental and physical edge. To be clear, that means still wearing a T-shirt and gym shorts, but they are strategic, intentionally chosen ones.

There is a challenge to this piece of the puzzle that I'll guide you through. I've analyzed a lot of wardrobes over the years, and there's always a common problem. When it comes to clothing, people buy what they like, not necessarily what they need or what will change their results.

Just yesterday, I was in the closet of a high-level executive who loves to go hunting. He loves to buy hunting jackets and pants, and he has many of them. The trouble is, he only goes hunting a few times a year. He has nothing to wear for everyday activities like dinner with his wife.

His shopping habits were acting against his decision to consistently look and feel great each day. He couldn't maintain his edge because he didn't have what he needed to do that in all the sectors of his life.

Let me give you a personal example. I love high heels. I like the way they look, and most of all, I like the way I feel in them. Specifically, they make me feel glamorous, sexy, and fun. However, 90% of my life doesn't make wearing high heels realistic. It's easy for me to buy them until I realize they aren't going to help me create the image I want with everyday consistency. Yes, I wear high heels, but when I know I can't, I have to figure out an alternative consistent with my overall image and how high heels make me feel. I channel how I feel in high heels (glamorous, sexy, and fun) and find a solution that gives me the same mental edge, whether a fun sneaker or a sexy wedge.

Don't Sell Yourself Short

In my opinion, the biggest reason people walk around selling themselves short by ignoring the edge they can create is that they think it has to be hard to look and feel good. They think, all of a sudden, it would take an enormous amount of time and effort before you could leave the house. What could be worse than trying to do that every day!?

This chapter can excite you about landing opportunities to rebuild your future, but at the end of the day, you'll change nothing if you think that dressing in a way that makes you look and feel good sounds miserable to maintain. I'd recommend that you don't change a thing about your image if you're not willing to maintain it.

Don't worry. Creating an edge takes a focused but small amount of effort, and maintaining it is easy. One of my newer clients recently texted me and said she couldn't believe how easy it was to dress for a date night. She said she was amazed at how everything in her closet made her look and feel good. We did some preparation together, but now her closet allows her to dress easily for many occasions.

I've found that most things worth doing require a little work on the front end to get the desired result on the other side. As I mentioned at the beginning of this formula piece, all it takes to get the result is to look and feel a certain way to achieve your desired result. What's your decision?

Chapter Four
Focusing on Health Post-Divorce

By: Dr. Aixa Goodrich

My mission is to improve lives, and I have been doing this for more than 20 years in my Functional Medicine and Chiropractic Wellness practice. One common theme I have seen with chronic health issues is that stress plays a significant role.

Stress comes in many different forms. There is good stress and bad stress. Stress is also physical, environmental, and mental/emotional. Physical stressors are injuries, accidents, falls, pregnancies, and traumas. Environmental stressors are chemical exposures, toxins in our food and water supply, and overuse of drugs, prescribed and recreational. Emotional or mental stress can be losing a loved one, job loss, financial issues, divorce, etc.

It's important to note that positive stress is also a real thing. For example, the birth of a child, graduation, job promotion, a new relationship, finalized divorce, or going rock climbing for the first time can be positive forms of stress. As you can see, stress can be positive or negative, depending on the situation.

The issue with negative stress is that a cascade of chemical reactions occurs in the body. There are five stages to the stress response: alarm, resistance, possible recovery, adaptation, and burnout.

The <u>alarm response</u> is the moment you first feel stressed. It fires up the alarm and sets your adrenal glands into motion. Your heart rate increases, as does your blood pressure. This stage is intended to solve an immediate problem.

The <u>resistance</u> or damage control stage bridges the stressor and your body's natural ability to return to homeostasis or balance. You can enhance and speed up this process by movement, i.e., exercise, which we will discuss further.

In recovery, you will likely feel physically and mentally exhausted and need rest and relaxation.

Many don't take or even have the time to recover from a stressful situation. In this adaptation stage, you may find yourself constantly on edge, overreacting in seemingly benign situations, experiencing physical symptoms, and suffering from depression and anxiety.

The last stage is burnout. You may find that you are alienating yourself from others and your daily responsibilities, experiencing chronic physical and emotional symptoms and difficulty concentrating and doing menial tasks.

When the body is stressed, the nervous system sets off your "fight or flight" response. The adrenal glands, two small glands on top of your kidneys, will release a flood of stress hormones known as cortisol and adrenaline/epinephrine, which prepare the body for emergency action. Heart rate increases, muscles tighten, blood pressure rises, and senses sharpen.

One key factor in understanding is that the body doesn't know the difference between a real and imagined threat. Our bodies will physically react and prepare us to go into survival mode. The body can't tell the difference between the stress of a saber tooth tiger coming at you to devour you and make you its next gourmet meal and you imagining the attack coming towards you from your ex, ex's lawyer, ex's family, etc. The cascade of stress hormones is released in both situations.

Chronic exposure to stress can have detrimental effects on your health. Adrenaline elevates your blood pressure and heart rate; cortisol, the primary stress hormone, increases blood sugar. Over time, if uncontrolled, the stress hormones can and will disrupt almost all bodily functions, putting you at risk of anxiety, depression, digestive issues, migraines, heart disease, weight gain, insomnia, and cognitive impairment.

Therefore, it is crucial to your health to have a coping mechanism. Otherwise, you will begin to see a decline in your overall health and well-being, as stress often leads to poor choices. It can be challenging to concentrate and think clearly when under pressure. When stressed out or going through a difficult situation, most people turn to alcohol and tobacco. They may overeat and even resort to drugs (prescribed and/or recreational).

Here are a few signs and symptoms of emotional stress that you should be aware of:

1. Chest pain/heaviness
2. Neck pain, back pain, and headaches
3. Shortness of breath and dizziness
4. Difficulty sleeping
5. Jaw clenching
6. Difficulty concentrating
7. Withdrawal

While it may seem that there is little you can do to alleviate your current life events and stressful situations, there are steps you can take to curb its detrimental effects.

Change Your Mindset

First, understand that everything is temporary, and this, too, shall pass. If you think about it, you've made it through 100% of the challenges that life has thrown at you. It's crucial to your mental well-being to focus on the desired outcome. Keeping your eye on the prize will help you focus on achieving a positive result without being overly distracted by minor setbacks. Getting sucked into the mundane details of a life-altering situation such as divorce is easy. Let your legal team deal with that.

I would strongly urge you to work on your mindset as well. A negative filter can exaggerate or exacerbate a negative situation. Focus on the positive aspects; something is always positive, even if you don't see it. How often have you told yourself, "What the hell was I thinking," after something was over, but during the thick of it, you couldn't see it? I'm a big believer that everything happens for a reason. Everything that happens in your life is an opportunity for you to grow and learn.

Sometimes the lessons are extremely painful, but you can use those lessons to help others who are going through similar experiences.

Prioritize Your Health with Exercise

Secondly, make your health a priority. Exercise is at the top of the list. Movement changes your state. It releases endorphins, the feel-good hormone and natural pain killer. You choose your exercise. It can be running, walking, dancing, weight training, swimming, yoga, etc. Exercise in any form improves your mood. It also increases your self-confidence, promotes relaxation, and lowers the symptoms of depression and anxiety. It also helps to reduce cortisol levels. Exercise is meditation in motion. If you are having difficulty getting up and exercising, recruit a buddy. Having someone hold you accountable is quite helpful.

Eat Healthier

Next, clean up your diet. That means fewer processed foods and more of a whole foods diet. The goal is to eat foods that decrease inflammation, reducing cortisol levels. A well-balanced diet can help boost your immune system, which is affected during stressful events. It also repairs damaged cells and provides extra energy to cope with stress.

You want to avoid sugar or sugary foods like cake, cookies, sodas, energy drinks, artificial sweeteners, and seed oils such as soybean, corn, canola, sesame, sunflower, and grape seed oils. For some, you should also avoid dairy and gluten, as they can be highly inflammatory. You want a meal plan with healthy proteins such as grass-fed beef, wild-caught fish, wild game, and free-range organic chicken. It should also include healthy fats like nuts and seeds, avocados, olive oil, coconut oil, and fatty fish. Half of your plate should be veggies, leafy green veggies. These are loaded with fiber and nutrients, which will keep you satiated and prevent things like constipation and heart disease and help lower cholesterol. Low glycemic fruit can also be good and help curb a sweet tooth.

Understandably, you may not be motivated to cook daily while going through stressful events. If this is the case, I would meal prep or sign up with a meal prep company to give you easy access to healthy options. It will deter you from opting for fast food or not eating, which is as bad. You'll also be less likely to binge on ice cream, cookies, chips, or comfort food. Having food readily available will keep you eating more regularly. Eating regularly helps keep your blood sugar stable and cortisol levels balanced. It'll also keep your mind alert and your energy levels even.

Decrease or eliminate caffeine which can make you anxious and even disrupt sleep. Get at least seven to nine hours of sleep. Many great, natural herbs can help with sleep disruption. Also, let us not forget to hydrate. Drinking half of your body weight in ounces will keep you hydrated, relieve constipation, and flush out toxins. (It will also keep you busy going #1, distracting you from all the stress.)

Practice Self-Love

When was the last time you did something good and fun for yourself? When was the last time you had a massage? Gift yourself a massage. Get chiropractic adjustments regularly as it regulates your nervous system, eases pain, and releases endorphins, the feel-good hormone.

Supplement your diet. So many of my patients have vitamin and nutrient deficiencies and don't even know about them. It's essential to know your levels. A vitamin D deficiency can lower your immune system, making you more prone to cancer, dementia, and osteoporosis. A deficiency in B vitamins can alter your mood, cause neurological symptoms, and affect your sleep patterns. Essential fatty acids regulate your immune and central nervous system and boost brain function. Essential fatty acids are not synthesized and must be consumed through diet or supplementation. Diet is always the best way to consume them. I run simple tests on my overly stressed patients and those going through difficult situations that help me identify how I can support them nutritionally.

A host of adaptogenic herbs and vitamins can help manage a healthy stress response during difficult times.

Journaling or Practicing Gratitude

Journaling can help identify the blessings in your life. What is working in your life right now? It's never all doom and gloom. What are you thankful for? Who are you grateful for? Journaling is a great tool to use daily. It can help you sort out your thoughts and feelings. I suggest counseling if your thoughts are overwhelming or need clarity or closure. Sometimes we seek the advice of friends and family to help us sort out our thoughts and feelings, and although they often mean well, they can give polarizing advice. A consultation with a professional and expert in that area will be more beneficial and effective in helping you get to a better place.

Seek Medical Assistance

Lastly, stressful situations often may have you seeking your doctor's help. The usual treatment is medication, and while certain cases may require this intervention, many do not. Meds help to suppress symptoms. However, if specific issues are not dealt with, they can worsen over time and cause more serious physical and emotional harm.

A Functional Medicine approach is the best choice for people with ongoing stress and stress-related conditions as it aims to treat the person instead of suppressing the symptoms. Functional medicine acknowledges the multi-factor causes like lifestyle choices, systemic imbalances such as gut and hormones, and traumas that haven't yet healed. It is essential to work with a physician who follows a holistic and inclusive approach while running the appropriate diagnostic testing to determine how they can best help you.

I'll share a story about a patient who came to me burnt out, tired, and fatigued. She was a walking zombie. She had not slept a full night in months, had gained 30 pounds, and was depressed and riddled with anxiety. While going through her health history, it was clear that she had experienced several stressful circumstances. She tragically lost a child a few years before and blamed herself. She worked long hours in a very stressful environment. She was surviving on caffeine and sugar. This took a toll on her health and her marriage. Her physical and mental health was a serious concern. She visited her PCP for help. They told her that she should get on anxiety and depression medication.

They also ran some labs and discovered that her thyroid was a bit off, her blood pressure was slightly elevated, and she was borderline diabetic. They offered her some meds to stabilize her, but she inherently knew that her lifestyle and mindset needed to change if she was going to regain her health.

The chronic stress had led to poor lifestyle choices, now affecting her health. She was in a dark place mentally. Her diet was poor. She was sleep-deprived. She was not exercising and had not dealt with significant past traumas.

I ran more comprehensive labs to check cortisol levels, food sensitivities, hormones, gut issues, and inflammation markers. She was somewhat shocked at the results and knew she was not well but didn't realize she was at a pivotal point.

We worked together on creating her goals of health first and foremost, but also what she wanted her life to look like going forward. This was a challenging process for her, as it is with most patients, as they have never sat down with their doctors to create a strategy, a plan, or a map, if you will. We developed an integrative program that included nutrition changes, exercise regimens, chiropractic adjustments, acupuncture, and mindset work with a holistic therapist. It took us six months to get her to a well-balanced and healthy state, but she is now thriving in her own business. She set up a charity in her child's name and renewed her relationship with her spouse.

This case was a woman, but this is a common theme in both women and men. Men are more likely to suffer from depression post-divorce than women. Research shows that men who go through divorce are more likely to develop heart disease and die at a younger age. That may be due to not having a strong support system, increased financial strains, inability to deal with emotions, and loss of identity. Men are expected to "MAN UP!" Men need help, too.

Health is a multifaceted phenomenon. It is a state of physical, emotional, and spiritual well-being, not merely the absence of disease or symptoms. A healthy body keeps you alive, active, and full of vitality. A healthy mind keeps you alert, focused, and engaged. A healthy soul/spirit keeps you fulfilled, grateful, and content. This is more of an Eastern concept and approach, which I think Western medicine seriously lacks. Regarding health, Eastern philosophies adopt a holistic conceptualization of an individual and his/her environment.

My hope for you is that you seek the help you need from a team of experts who take a holistic approach, from your doctor to your therapist and even your lawyer. It may seem that you are going through hell right now, but in the words of Winston Churchill, "If you're going through hell, keep going." Seriously, why would you want to stop there?

Chapter Five
Selling Your Most Valuable Asset in a Divorce

By: Carlos Gutierrez

We offer you this guide because we have seen the best and worst outcomes in these situations. The goal is to be able to avoid the problems before they occur. When negotiating the sale of my parents' house, it was also embroiled in a divorce. My mother has had a very rapid decline in her Alzheimer's condition. This set my stepfather down a path toward a nervous breakdown. To add more complexity to the mix, they have a special needs daughter, my sister, and their relationship as husband and wife has been lost for years. They are fortunate to have a family member who has gotten clients through this hundreds of times.

Our team has seen this numerous times before. It's important to understand each case is different, yet one thing remains the same: You must hire the right professionals. Further, even more impactful, is the fact that so many things can go wrong. What do you do when you have people and processes causing complexities that affect your home sale? Read on.

Typically, in any life event, divorce being no exception, the family home is the largest asset in the transition. Listing and selling property are complex matters without a divorce looming, so a divorce's added complexity and emotional factor make it even more delicate.

If you are reading this book, you are likely no stranger to how stressful and complex it is to deal with a divorce. If you pile on to that selling a home, you must be extra careful, as there are tons of pitfalls and possible mistakes that will make your life even more difficult. In divorce and in any contentious real estate sale, for that matter, we must worry about the people involved as much as processes, incase not everyone's goals are aligned. Effectively navigating people and processes takes skill. While I'll outline the best technical steps in selling a home through a divorce, it's important to acknowledge that the problem is rarely the technical part of selling a home. The biggest problem is the divorce itself and how the parties involved can get in their own way.

It is crucial to surround yourself with a team that is highly detail-oriented, experienced and, above all, patient. It takes a tremendous amount of patience to successfully navigate a home sale and a divorce. If the emotions are yours, then the professionals around you should be familiar with the need to quell the rises and falls of the emotional roller coaster so that they can efficiently remove the emotional part from where it doesn't belong throughout the process.

Some Questions You Should Ask Yourself:

1. What are the financial ramifications of selling a home before, during, or after the divorce?

2. How do I pick the right expert to help with this process?

3. How do I best prepare my kids and my mindset for the sale?

4. How should I prepare the home for a fast and profitable sale?

Before getting into the answers to those questions, let's cover some of the basic mechanics of a sale.

The "Note" is the document that outlines the debt you agreed to incur in exchange for a mortgage.

The "Deed" is the equivalent of the title of the home. You can be an owner on a deed without being a borrower on the mortgage. You can also be on the mortgage debt as well as the deed. Both scenarios are common.

Your finances will depend on figuring out into which category you fall. Florida's homestead laws still have some provisions protecting spouses who are married and own a primary residence. Remember that there are different implications for selling an investment property that is not your primary home, so please consult your attorney on the differences.

The "mortgage" is the document that pledges the home as collateral. The most important part of future financial planning will come from the "mortgage payoff" and the home's sale price.

You should call or message your lender to request a "payoff statement" and your home insurer to find out who the listed beneficiaries of the policy are. The payoff will provide the needed amount to pay off all the mortgage debt, interest, fees, penalties, and any escrow advances the lender has paid on your behalf. You will subtract the payoff amount from the sale price to get the net proceeds you can expect for the home after closing costs. Your attorney can advise on the best way to request that the funds be divided between the parties.

In an amicable divorce, a sale can happen if all property owners agree to sell, which REALTOR® to hire, an initial sale price, and how funds will be disbursed. No special permission to sell is required. However, depending on the stage of your divorce, you must consult your family law attorney to ensure the courts do not need to grant permission on any of these factors.

Most of the following will cover some of the best practices in a home sale when there is a contentious situation. It is crucial to try to take emotion out of the picture of the home sale in the divorce. This is, of course, easier said than done. However, it is a given that the most prepared party will come out ahead in any situation. Being prepared with the knowledge this reading provides will immediately put you ahead of the curve.

Couples can reside in the home together during the divorce; consult your attorney to establish the legal and financial ramifications of moving out of the home before the completion of the divorce.

How do I prepare financially for the sale?

It is crucial to begin to plan as early into the process as possible. Even if the relationship is reconciled and the divorce is canceled at some point, being armed with financial knowledge will set you up for financial success.

Begin with the basics of writing down all of your debts and all of your assets. Suppose you have not yet engaged a real estate professional. You can look on the internet for sales of homes that are similar to yours in size, remodel condition, and proximity, but getting in touch with a professional is always best. This is a very basic method, but it is the same one that appraisers will follow in great detail. Avoid assuming websites such as Zillow have an accurate picture of your home's value. They are machine algorithms that could never replace the expertise of an experienced real estate agent.

Now you can order the aforementioned "payoff". Several calculators online will help you by inputting an estimated sale price, date, and payoff and then providing you with a net proceed amount. They will automatically deduct the closing costs a seller must pay, such as Deed Tax, title insurance, commissions, etc. This net number is more important than the sale price.

It is important to note the financial ramifications of selling before, during, or after the divorce. You can choose any of these, but they have advantages and complexities.

In Florida, if you sell before divorcing, the couple is exempt from a capital gain of up to $500,000 for the sale of a primary, not investment, home. If you sell during the divorce proceeding, you will receive the same benefit, but now the process may need to be approved by the courts and the attorneys involved. In short, the capital gain is similar to long-term profit. You subtract today's price from what you bought the home for, minus the expenses to improve the home. The resulting gain above $500,000.00 is taxed as a long-term capital gain.

If you sell the home after the divorce, you are each entitled to only $250,000 in exemptions from gains. This assumes you have occupied the home as a primary home in two of the last five years. Consulting with a knowledgeable accountant can help understand any tax liabilities from selling the home before or after the divorce.

Preparing your finances also includes preparing your credit. It is crucial, if possible, to continue paying the mortgage, taxes, insurance, and especially any homeowners association dues throughout the divorce process.

We enter a separate arena of problems if there are delinquent mortgage payments. Late mortgage payments (30 days or more) negatively impact your credit. This will hurt your prospects of getting a future mortgage or even a rental once you are ready to move. If you are in this situation, then to some extent, the damage is done, and you must mitigate any future consequences. Call your mortgage company and ask how far behind the mortgage is and if you can pay or reinstate the loan into good standing.

How do I pick the right professionals to work with?

Regarding real estate and lending professionals, it is important to have a thorough interview if you do not have any first-hand background knowledge of their abilities and experience. Consider the source of the referral. Was it someone you clicked on from the internet? Was it a referral by a trusted friend? In the best cases, has your attorney recommended someone with whom they have worked in the past? Our team has been appointed by the judges in family court when neither the divorcing parties nor their attorneys can agree on which professional will list the home for sale.

Avoid going with a real estate agent because they are your friend. We have seen this mistake many times. First, it can affect the friendship. Second, your relationship does not dictate their ability to sell a home well nor the ability to handle a delicate and complex scenario such as divorce. The divorcing parties must both feel comfortable with the REALTOR® to avoid the misinterpretation that the REALTOR® works with one of the two parties' best interests in mind.

A quick note on REALTORS®: A licensed real estate agent is not a REALTOR® unless they are a member of the National Association of REALTORS®. REALTORS® must abide by a code of ethics, which non- REALTOR® agents do not. Some REALTORS® have been trained to work with divorce's legal, tax, and emotional implications.

I have led one of the chapters of the National Association of Divorce Professionals, which offers various resources for divorcing couples. Despite your home sale originating from a divorce, your listing agent does not need to disclose this to potential buyers. Your motivation to sell is not something that is required to be disclosed. An agent experienced in divorce sales should easily navigate the best way to answer this when asked.

What about the kids?

First, to ease the children through a home transition, get them involved. Whether it's to a two-home situation or a downgrade in home size, include them in the decisions if this is age appropriate. Take them to see potential homes and paint a picture of what it would look like if they lived there. Let them pick their rooms and plan improvements, such as a playground if there is a yard in the home you will be occupying.

Second, consider having your real estate professional not use a lock box on the front door for showings and access to the home you are selling. This reminds children daily that they are losing their childhood home. The side of the house or out of site should be ok as an alternative. The same can be said for a "For Sale" sign. This is not to say that the answer is avoidance, but a daily reminder is unnecessary.

This process is painful for everyone, but it is a necessary one in order to move on to the next stage of life.

I recommend searching for a documentary named *Split—A Film for Kids of Divorce (and their parents)*. It lays out candid interviews with kids who have gone through divorce. You would learn that most kids experience and perceive divorce quite differently. There are levels of understanding and acceptance that run the full spectrum and the full range of emotions. The documentary is very enlightening.

Prepping the House

Preparing the house for sale in a divorce is no different from a regular sale. Here are some of the basics.

- Clean. You must wake up every day the house is listed with the mentality, "This is the day the buyer will be coming through the door."

- Deep clean the home, then keep daily cleaning as a priority.

- Declutter. We decorate our homes to our comfort, not to appeal to the next person who might buy them. You must put yourself in the position of a buyer and clear out as much as possible to show your home's true size, space, and potential.

- Remove all the unnecessary and overly personal furniture and touches. Remove excessive family photos. The buyer needs to imagine themselves living in the home and not that you still live in it and will be leaving soon. Depersonalizing is key.

- Staging is not always necessary and involves removing your furniture from the house. However, if the house is already vacant or you don't mind moving twice, effective staging can make a home more appealing to the buyer and, in some cases, net you more money.

- The same goes for curb appeal. If you can clean up landscaping, paint old fences, and patch any holes, you will go a long way to boost your home sale regarding price and time.

- Neutral colors are much easier on the eye than bright colors or outdated wall coverings. Make sure to paint in neutral colors if time and funds allow.

- We don't typically recommend remodeling right before selling. It adds expense that you might not recoup in the form of a return on investment and will certainly add time and complexity to the process. However, if you feel you must make upgrades, then focus on the biggest money-makers: kitchens, baths, and landscaping.

Finally, remember that, like most things in life, a home sale follows the 80/20 rule. The buyer has to fall in love with 20% of the house to accept the rest. This can be something eye-catching or of great comfort, such as a lush backyard, a pool, a fireplace, or a magnificent view. Whatever made you fall in love with the home might be the same aspect the next buyer will love.

Chapter Six

Real Estate, Divorce, and Death: Where Business Meets Emotion

By: Alina Nuñez, Esq.

When you think of real estate, the first thing that probably pops into your head is the picture of a beautiful home or maybe a building or a piece of land, but it is so much more complicated than that. Different aspects of life are intertwined with our real estate. Marriage, divorce, and death are a few. In the next few pages, you will explore some common issues you can face in these different scenarios.

Moving is one of life's stressful events. First, there's finding the right place. Then there's the packing and unpacking, finding new schools, and new neighbors, along with any financial stressors. There is also the emotional stress of moving, especially if you've been in a place for a long time and have to start fresh in a new neighborhood, city, or even country. Then add to that DIVORCE.

Divorce ranks as life's second most stressful event, and decisions over what to do with the family house drive some of the most heated disputes between couples parting ways. Even if both partners agree on ending the relationship, several emotional, practical, and legal considerations must be dealt with, such as living arrangements, financial matters, and child custody.

Beyond the emotional ties to a home, shared real estate has an intricate maze of legal strings that must be sorted out before the dust can settle. It's a bit more complicated than splitting up the wedding china.

Are you getting divorced? Do you worry about what will happen with your family home or any other property you own jointly? Should you sell it, buy out your spouse's share, or have them buy yours? What are your options? You need answers to these questions about real estate and divorce, and to reduce your uncertainty about your post-divorce future, you want those answers fast! You can find workable solutions to your housing and other issues during divorce with your cooperation, patience, and assistance from family law and real estate lawyers.

Real Estate and Divorce Question #1: Should I Sell the House?

Divorce brings a lot of changes, especially when considering whether to sell your family home or not. You have to take into consideration if you are going to uproot your children, move them from the home they grew up in and cause further changes during an already difficult time. If emotions are high and it's difficult to have a conversation or reach an agreement, some laws can force a particular outcome. The decision to keep or sell the house is emotional and financial. Sometimes our wants aren't financially feasible, especially regarding the outcome of the house. This is why cooperation goes a long way in this situation.

- Deciding to sell depends on your answers to the following questions:

- Does it make sense to continue to hold the title with your ex-spouse? Maybe the real estate market is down, and not the best time to sell.

- Can you keep paying the mortgage and maintenance by yourself?

- How long would you live in the house if you kept it?

- What or how much would you give up by keeping it?

- Are you willing to sign up for any tax consequences if you keep it?

An important question I often ask is whether you have to disclose to any potential buyer that you are getting divorced. You have no legal obligation to disclose your divorce to buyers, and you should work with an agent you trust to be discreet and safeguard your confidential information. Keep any evidence of turmoil private, and do whatever you can to avoid unintentionally airing your dirty laundry. Your divorce does not affect the buyers.

One of the best ways to keep your divorce private is to ensure the home looks tidy from the outside in and remains in generally sellable condition. Property in disrepair will send red flags to buyers that there's trouble at home, which they may try to use as leverage in negotiations. *A regular home sale… nothing to see here, folks!*

Ensure your curb appeal gets a refresh (99% of Realtors recommend it), so mow the lawn, trim the hedges, touch up any chipped or peeling paint, and brush away debris and grime from the front entrance. On the inside, the home needs to stay clean, depersonalized and decluttered throughout the entire home sale process.

Even when emotions are at an all-time high, you must treat selling your home like a business deal and follow your real estate agent's advice regarding home preparations, including cleaning, decluttering, and staging. The alternative is accepting an offer lower than what your home is worth. Maybe immediately selling is not the best answer, but these things must be considered and discussed. The timing of that sale could mean more money in your pocket the day you walk away.

Real Estate and Divorce Question #2: Should I Consider Buying Out My Spouse?

If selling is not the best option, then buying out the other person's interest is one way of dealing with a family home in a divorce. The custodial parent commonly buys out the non-custodial parent's interest for kids to keep living in the house. This way, the kids can remain in the home that they are familiar with and cause as little disruption to their lives in an already difficult situation.

In a situation where one spouse buys out the other spouse's interest in the home, many factors must be considered. First, an appraisal of the property will need to be done to determine the home's true value. Once you've determined the value of your home, subtract the amount you owe on your mortgage from your home's value and divide the result by two. This will tell you how much equity each of you probably has.

If there is a current mortgage on the home, and especially if the loan is in the name of the ex-spouse who is selling their share, then the one keeping the home would have to qualify for a new mortgage to pay off the old mortgage and remove the ex-spouse from the loan. Transferring the title or ownership of the home does not modify or change the existing loan. This can be challenging when all your assets, including your savings, are split during the divorce. Of course, the spouse assuming ownership will need the necessary income and credit score to qualify for the new loan. The process gets more complicated if a divorcing couple is underwater on their home, meaning they owe more on the house than it's currently worth or face financial hardship.

Also, if you don't have the credit and income to qualify for a loan, this might not be the best option for you. Often in a divorce, the parties will agree that the spouse remaining in the home will have to refinance within a certain period, one to two years, to remove the ex-spouse from the loan and allow them time to repair their credit or save money to qualify for a new loan. These are all important factors to consider.

Getting your name off the deed is easy, but not off the mortgage. If not impossible, it might make it harder for you to leave your name on the mortgage when applying for a loan to buy your new home. Both of you can ruin your credit score fast if one of you takes the title, but both of you are still on the mortgage. Also, if the spouse who's keeping the house isn't able to make the mortgage payments, your credit score will be negatively affected.

Real Estate and Divorce Question #3: Should I Buy a New House?

You have started the divorce process, hired your attorney, and filed the paperwork to start the case. You are ready to move on with your life and get a jump start on the future. Maybe that new future involves buying a new home. One important thing to consider is that until you have that Final Judgment of Dissolution of Marriage, you are still "legally" married. Any new property that you were to purchase would still be as a married person and could raise issues with your ex-spouse. If you buy a property before your divorce is finalized, your ex-spouse will likely have to sign off on certain documents for the closing. Also, your ex can claim an interest in your new home if you didn't purchase it as a separate property.

I cannot tell you how many times I have had a buyer tell me that they were "divorced" while under contract to purchase a property, and when I ask them for a copy of their Final Judgment of Dissolution of Marriage, they tell me, "Well, the process isn't finished yet." My response is always the same: "Until the judge signs the Final Judgment, you are still married to your ex-spouse, no matter how much you hate them." Now you risk losing the escrow deposit given for the new home if you can't close on the purchase. One time, I had a buyer in this situation, and luckily, we were able to negotiate a 30-day extension with the seller to speed up the divorce and get the Final Judgment signed by the judge and close. It was not the ideal situation, but we got it done.

Another common situation is when an individual buys a property and never files for divorce because they have been separated from their spouse for several years. In their mind, they are "single." NO! You are still married! It doesn't matter if you have been separated for a day or 20 years; if there is no signed Final Judgment of Dissolution of marriage, you are still legally married.

Consult an experienced lawyer about how these actions could negatively impact you or for ways to ensure that they *can't* come back to haunt you before embarking on making an offer on a new home before your divorce is finalized.

Real Estate and Divorce Question #3: What If My Ex Refuses to Sell?

You may sell the home in a divorce, but your ex-spouse won't cooperate. If your ex-spouse can't afford to buy you out, you must work with your divorce attorney to file a partition action with a family law judge and compel the sale. You will need that signed court order to sign any contract for the sale of the property, the deed, and any other closing documents needed to transfer ownership to the new buyer.

Real Estate and Divorce Question #4: What Happens to Our Mortgage in a Divorce?

Normally, if the home is not sold due to the divorce, one spouse must make the monthly mortgage payments. However, if the spouse required to make payments fails to pay, both parties may still be liable to the bank. If both parties signed the promissory note, the divorce settlement would not extinguish a spouse's obligation to the bank. The bank is not a party to the divorce case and did not consent to any such agreement. Instead, the spouse must seek indemnification from the party required to pay under the divorce settlement agreement.

The spouse remaining in the house must refinance the mortgage in their name. Otherwise, if they remain on the mortgage, they can still be liable to the bank even if they no longer own the property. If you are the spouse giving up their rights to the home, you must ensure your name is removed from the loan before you sign off on the deed. Removing your name from the deed or title to the home does <u>not</u> remove your name from the loan.

Real Estate and Divorce Question #5: What Happens If One Spouse Dies Before Divorce Is Final?

You're in the middle of your divorce, and the unexpected happens: Your ex dies. Now what? Since a judge signs no Final Judgment, you are still considered legally married. Since the divorce was not finalized, the surviving spouse will probably have the right to inherit property from the deceased person's estate. Under Florida law, the surviving spouse will inherit the deceased spouse's marital estate if no minor children are involved, even if the decedent's will says otherwise. If the spouses share children, the surviving spouse will be granted the marital home until death.

Real Estate and Divorce Question #6: What Happens If I Die After My Divorce Is Final?

Many people will execute a will to provide for their family upon death. Most will give their spouse top priority to receive all or most of the assets of their estate upon death, which is a common way for spouses to provide for their partners. However, 50 percent of all marriages in the United States will end in divorce. If you die after a divorce and never update your will, and the will continues to name an ex-spouse, an important question becomes, "Does the ex-spouse receive a portion of the estate?"

Florida law is clear that provisions in a will in favor of the ex-spouse are revoked. Your will is not automatically void upon divorce, and your estate will pass under the provisions set out within it, but it will be treated as if your ex-spouse had died during your lifetime. This means that any appointments as executor or trustee will fail, and any gifts for your ex-spouse's benefit will also fail. If your spouse was the sole beneficiary of your will, then your estate will pass under the rules of intestacy.

You must also update your will for any property gained or lost during the divorce. If you have assets specifically identified in your will, update them for any changes due to the divorce.

The important items to update in your will are your beneficiaries, executor, property, and guardianship of minor children. If you have children with your ex-spouse, you will want to update your will to appoint a guardian in the unlikely event that you and your ex-spouse are unavailable to raise your children. In the event of your untimely death, your children will most likely be raised by your ex-spouse.

Making decisions about the family home adds complexity to an already stressful process. Still, the key takeaway is that whatever path you choose, let it be for your long-term financial interests rather than a heat-of-moment win. Along with your family lawyer, your real estate lawyer can help smooth out the divorce process for you, review all the documents, and ensure that all legal undertakings are executed properly.

Chapter Seven

Financial Advice from an Investment Adviser Representative

By: Liliana De Lara

A large percentage of US marriages end in divorce. While you do not get married thinking that you will probably end up divorced, there are some things you can do to prepare financially once the worst-case scenario seems very likely to happen.

Divorce can be a complicated and confusing journey. It is important to envision your ideal future, avoid financial pitfalls, and find an answer to some questions that may be lingering in your mind:

1. Will I be okay financially?

2. Can I afford to pay the mortgage and all the household expenses?

3. What should I do with my investments?

4. Will I ever be able to retire?

While financial planning due to divorce is not much different from financial planning in general, some things must be taken into consideration that are specific to persons getting a divorce.

Financial planning due to divorce focuses on developing financial strategies that can help you get back on your feet after the divorce and recover any lost financial ground before you are no longer able or want to work.

Everything may seem overwhelming at this point. I am going to suggest two simple steps:

1. Get Organized!

Start by collecting your joint financial information, including the most recent statements from banks, credit cards, brokerage accounts, employer retirement accounts [401(k), 403(b)], any loans or debt, insurance, mortgage, pensions, social security statements, income tax returns, and any other pertinent financial documents.

Do you have paper statements? Do you have online access to these documents? It is a good idea to securely keep a digital copy of all your records. If you are struggling with where some accounts or assets are located, your Investment Adviser Representative can help you. Make sure you have access to all joint account information.

Document all property: real estate, cars, boats, etc. Document all household goods, especially those with sentimental value or financially valuable. Gather any receipts you have or find out what the replacement value is. Take pictures.

Do you currently have a budget? You will need to update it to figure out how much income you need to cover all your fixed expenses once you become the head of your household. I have attached one in the appendix of this book. You may make copies. If you wish for a complimentary electronic version, please contact me.

2. Assemble a Team

It is important to rely on advice from professionals, not from well-intentioned family members, friends, acquaintances, and members of Facebook groups that you belong to. While they may have the best intentions, they may not know the laws in your state and are also not privy to your whole financial picture to give you adequate advice.

You may have heard that you should not make important financial decisions in haste while going through a very difficult time in your life, as you may later regret them. While it is true that some decisions can and should be postponed, there are some you need to tackle head-on before the divorce decree is final.

Build a support team of professionals who will help guide you on your financial journey through and even past divorce. Here are some of the divorce professionals you may need depending on your circumstances:

- Family Law Attorney

- QDRO attorney (Qualified Domestic Relations Order)

- Tax Adviser

- CDFA (Certified Divorce Financial Analyst)

- Investment Adviser Representative

- Life coach

- Therapist

- Health Insurance Agent

- Image Consultant

- Health Practitioner

- Estate Planning Attorney

- Banker

- Credit Repair Specialist

- Personal Injury Attorney

- Parenting Coordinator

- Realtor

- Home Staging Specialist

- Home Inspector

- Appraiser

- Mortgage Broker

- Business Valuator

- Insurance Agent

- Forensic Accountant

- Private Investigator

- Bankruptcy Attorney

- Career Counselor

Having the right people around you could make all the difference. Once you add the first couple of professionals to your team, they can refer you to the others as needed.

The role of an Investment Adviser Representative is to guide you so you can make decisions based on facts and knowledge, not emotions. Trusting that your Investment Adviser Representative has your best interest at heart is important.

You will want to make decisions that you will not regret later. Things can go wrong when you allow emotions to cloud your judgment.

If you already have a financial plan, implementing some important changes will probably be necessary. The sooner you do it, the sooner you can get back on track and the better the potential future outcome for your financial health.

The eight pillars of a holistic financial plan are:

I. Retirement Planning:

As you split the household in two, some of the most important things that need to be split are the retirement assets: Pensions, 401(k)s, 457 Deferred Compensation accounts, 403(b)s, 401(a), SIMPLE IRAs, SEP IRAs, IRAs. Except for IRAs, you will need a Qualified Domestic Relations Order (QDRO) to split all the other retirement assets. Not all family law attorneys draw up QDROs, but your attorney will be the best person to recommend someone for the QDRO if they don't personally handle them.

Even if you get half of your marital retirement assets, remember they will be funding not half but 100% of your expenses in retirement. You need a Financial Plan to determine if you are on target to retire at the age you originally intended.

It is important to do it now and not wait until you are getting ready to retire. A shortfall is much easier to address if you are ten years away

from retirement than ten days away. Whatever
figure you had in your plan or mind will
probably not work now that you must pay for
all the household expenses and any unexpected
expenses that may come your way with only
your income and assets.

The financial and retirement challenge will be
greater the closer you are to retirement, as there
will be very little time to make up for the lost
ground. Most of the plans you had in place
previously will no longer work. If you bought a
second home in anticipation of retirement, who
would keep it? Who will keep the home if you
have been paying down the mortgage to retire
mortgage-free? Will you have to take out a new
mortgage to give your ex-spouse his/her
equitable share, or will you be moving out?

You should never knowingly get yourself into a
financial bind. If you cannot afford the
mortgage on your home with your income
alone, it may be time to consider other options.
I suggest you do not stretch your finances to
keep the house at the expense of long- and
short-term savings and investment goals. You
may want to consider getting bought out by

your soon-to-be ex-spouse or putting the house on the market for sale.

It is important to go over all the different financial scenarios before the negotiations start to negotiate from a position of strength and knowledge. It is difficult to modify the terms of the Marital Settlement Agreement (MSA)/Divorce Settlement Agreement once the divorce is finalized. Hence, reaching the best settlement possible before you reach that point is important.

II. Social Security Strategies:

There are many strategies for married couples to maximize their social security benefits. If your financial plan included any of them, you would probably have to scratch them off as your options are now different.

Understanding your projected social security benefits is important so they can be part of your planning.

You should obtain a current social security statement as soon as possible if you have not already done it. You can obtain it by logging into ssa.gov and clicking "My Social Security" to create an account. If you already have one, you can download your most recent statement. If you don't, you can create one. If you have further questions, call the Social Security Administration at 1-800-772-1213.

- If your marriage lasted at least ten years, you might be able to collect on your ex-spouse's record if you meet the following requirements:

- You are unmarried.

- You are age 62 or older.

- Your ex-spouse is entitled to social security retirement or disability benefits.

- The benefit you are entitled to receive based on your work record is less than the benefit you would receive based on your ex-spouse's work record.

If you meet these requirements, you may be entitled to receive full or unreduced benefits based on your ex-spouse's work record if you wait until full retirement age. Your full retirement age will vary depending on the year you were born. If you were born in 1960 or later, your full retirement age is 67. You can still receive reduced benefits starting at age 62. At full retirement age, the highest benefit you can receive for an ex-spouse's work record is 50%. You may also collect survivor benefits after your ex-spouse dies, even if she/he had remarried if you didn't remarry before turning 60.

If your ex-spouse's benefits exceed yours, several possible strategies should be considered carefully before deciding which benefit to take and when. One involves deciding whether to start receiving social security benefits at 62, full retirement age of 70, or any other time between 62 and 70. It should not be done without carefully weighing each alternative's pros and cons carefully with your Investment Adviser Representative. You can obtain more information by going to the ssa.gov website.

III. Estate Planning:

I would recommend you speak with an Estate Planning attorney regarding the following items:

Establishing an Estate Plan involves making several important and often difficult decisions. The key ones include the following:

- Who gets what assets and when?

- Guardianship of your minor and/or adult disabled child/children.

- End-of-life decisions: your Advanced Healthcare Medical Directive detailing how you want your end-of-life to be handled.

- Naming who you want to serve as your Power of Attorney.

- Naming a Trustee and Successor Trustee.

- Legacy: How do you want to be remembered?

- Asset Distribution: Who gets which assets and when?

1. If you already have all these documents in place, you will want to contact your estate planning attorney for any updates that will be needed:

2. Revocable living trust.

3. Durable Power of Attorney: one that "kicks in" and becomes valid if you become incapacitated.

4. Current or updated beneficiary designation forms for retirement accounts, life insurance policies, and investment accounts.

5. Specific bequests: Who gets what?

6. Advanced healthcare medical directives.

7. Complete transfer on death (TOD) forms on all bank accounts.

8. Ensure that any real estate holdings will transfer outright to the selected beneficiary through the deed.

IV. Tax Planning:

I recommend you also speak with a Tax Professional regarding the following:

1. Will you fulfill the IRS's head of household requirements?

2. Will you claim your children as dependents every year, every other year, or never?

3. Do you have investments in non-qualified accounts that are generating taxable income?

4. Could they be moved to a tax-deferred account?

5. Do you have money in retirement accounts to convert into Roth IRAs?

6. Would it be better to do it now, when you retire, or never?

This also requires careful planning. You should not make these decisions without talking to your Tax Adviser.

V. Medicare/Healthcare Planning:

1. Do you have health insurance through your employer?

2. Will you have to return to the workforce?

3. Were you expecting to be on your ex-spouse's workplace group health insurance until age 65?

4. Do you qualify for Medicare benefits on your work record?

5. Can you access healthcare through the Affordable Care Act (ACA)?

It is important to review the different options with your Health Insurance Agent.

VI. Life Insurance:

Are you the beneficiary of a life insurance policy on your ex-spouse? Were you counting on that money to provide for income when he died? Whether your ex-spouse decides on their own or through a court order to keep a current life insurance policy or buy a new one to provide for alimony or child support in case of premature death, it is important that you become the policy's owner. That way, you will be notified if your ex-spouse stops paying the policy, changes beneficiary, or reduces the face amount of the policy.

Have you considered the cash value inside a permanent policy as an asset that should be divided? It is also important to check for surrender charges before you cancel a life insurance policy.

There are several possible options regarding life insurance in a divorce, and you should go over them with a life insurance agent:

- You can keep the same policies you already have.

- If the policies have cash value, they can be cashed out, and the cash value, if it is considered a marital asset, can be divided among both spouses.

- If the court orders, you or your ex-spouse may be required to keep a life insurance policy in force as part of a settlement. It can be considered part of alimony or child support.

- A new policy may be issued to replace an existing policy because it aligns better with the needs of both sides going forward. For example, a whole life policy may be replaced with a term policy because coverage only needs to be in place for a specified amount of time, usually until children turn 18 or 21.

- Ownership of policies may and should sometimes be transferred from one spouse to the other for various reasons. One would be to ensure premiums continue to be paid, for example.

From a financial planning perspective, life insurance should be a part of any long-term financial plan. Divorce can complicate your insurance outlook in various ways. Your attorney and a licensed insurance agent can assist in addressing those issues.

VII. Lifetime Income Planning:

Lifetime income planning ensures you have a steady stream of income that lasts as long as you do. Since pension plans and social security benefits are becoming a smaller piece of the pie, some planning is required to make sure the amount of income you receive from your investments increases to compensate for the loss of purchasing power due to inflation. This means some assets may have to remain invested in the stock market even after you retire. To do this, you must be comfortable with the degree of risk that being partially invested in the stock market entails.

Some different options would be:

- Dividend-paying stocks.

- Designating a spend-down account.

- Laddered bond portfolio.

- Laddered CD portfolio.

- Stock options strategies.

- Annuities.

- Taking distributions from the cash value of a life insurance policy.

We often recommend using more than one of these strategies to diversify your portfolio.

VIII. Investment Management:

Who has made investment decisions in the past? Who has selected the individual investments? Who has an established relationship with an Investment Adviser Representative? Do you wish to manage your investments independently on top of everything you are doing right now? Would you like to work with an Investment

Adviser Representative who can help you mitigate the losses to your portfolio when the stock market is going down?

While even thinking of doing all these things may seem too burdensome, remember that you do not have to do it alone or at once. Start by assembling your support team of professionals who can guide you through it all.

Investment Adviser Representative of and advisory services offered through Royal Fund Management, LLC, an SEC Registered Adviser.

The content contained herein is for informational purposes only and does not constitute a solicitation or offer to sell securities or investment advisory services. Investments are not FDIC-insured or deposits of or guaranteed by a bank or any other entity, so they may lose value. Past performance does not guarantee future results, and clients should not assume that future performance will be comparable to past performance.

Our Form ADV Part 2A, a firm disclosure document, is available for review. Please call or email to request a copy. This document contains detailed information about Royal Fund Management, LLC and the services provided.

The information contained does not represent any advice from a legal or tax standpoint. The information is solely based on opinion, and you should always seek the guidance of a licensed professional.

Chapter Eight

Financial Matters to Consider Tied to Your Journey toward Dissolution of Marriage or Divorce

By: Fidel Fernandez

Being Prepared

I have been a Banker for over 38 years, hold degrees in Finance and Economics, and have held various licenses in the financial fields. I am also a divorcee. I can attest with certainty and through personal experience that we are not fully prepared to undertake divorce's financial complexities and uncertainties on our own. Securing expert guidance and legal counsel will ease the ambivalence, hesitation, uncertainty, and fear of the unknown future that a life-changing event such as a divorce brings to individuals.

Most fears caused by financial uncertainty are usually tied to poor planning before, during, and after a major life-altering event such as a divorce or catastrophic events such as illnesses or other major changes in your life. A financial professional and your attorney can create a plan to ease the stress associated with these events.

We all need coaching at some point in our lives, especially when our feelings are getting in the way of making clear financial and legal decisions. It is often said that only a fool represents themselves in a legal matter, and that can be extrapolated to many important areas of your life, such as your finances, when it comes to taking your feelings out of important decisions affecting your future. When our heart takes over what our brain should decide, we do not always make sound or seemingly good common-sense decisions for ourselves, our family, or our loved ones. This is the time to seek professional help and advice.

The fear of the unknown causes us stress, and a divorce can turn our lives upside down. This is especially true when we consider that we do not know what the future holds for our relationships or how our decisions will affect our family, friends, children, work, living arrangements, or overall quality of life in many cases. We have a right to be concerned about all the decisions we make at this point. This is where a great attorney and legal team with access to many resources can guide you through these tense moments. A law firm that is prepared to provide you with legal counsel and access to other close network resources in various fields becomes invaluable for your needs. A financial expert working with your attorney can provide a sense of control over your situation, ultimately providing security and peace of mind.

Four Major Areas to Consider in Our Financial Lives

Let's consider four major areas of our financial lives and how to prepare for them in a divorce. Assets, liabilities, income, and expenses will need special attention. What assets will you need? What are your liabilities to consider? Where do you derive or will derive your income from? What will your expenses look like in the short and long term?

You must consider the areas that will affect you, your spouse, and your dependents moving forward, including current, future, retirement planning, and investment options. It is extremely important to consider financial decisions early in the process. I recommend that, as soon as you decide the situation in your marriage is deteriorating, and before the situation comes to a level where dissolution becomes the only solution to your financial and emotional well-being, you begin to prepare a plan of action for your financial future. It is never early enough!

A dissolution may be the only way to move forward with your life, but it does not mean that, with proper preparation, you will not have a viable financial solution for everyone concerned. It may never be a bad idea at any point in your marriage to have various bank accounts to address your needs. I have found that having accounts separated into yours, theirs, and mutual accounts to share common expenses leads to less financial tension in a marriage. However, many marriages do quite well with commonly shared accounts, shared expenses, and shared decisions. I believe in being prepared for all eventualities.

When considering a divorce from a financial perspective, start by thinking about liquid assets such as checking accounts, cash on hand, savings accounts, money markets, precious metals that can be sold, and short-term investments that can be liquidated. This will help you plan how you will have access to immediate solutions for current needs.

Also, think of longer-term assets such as time deposits, CDs, annuities, stocks, bonds, timeshares, mutual funds, real estate, accounts held for minor children, school savings accounts, insurance policies, IRAs, and pension plans.

These are not all-inclusive lists of short-term or long-term assets, but they provide a starting point for you to consider, including tax consequences, such as taking immediate distributions or waiting further down the line when it becomes a lesser tax burden for you. This is where your attorney can suggest a partner and an expert in tax solutions as part of their partner resources for your case.

As mentioned previously, other things that you will need to consider will include living expenses, tax consequences of dissolving certain assets (long and short term), and penalties for dissolving certain assets such as CDs and annuities. Long-term assets, such as IRAs, work-related retirement accounts, insurance plans, pension plans, and 401(k)s, may all have individual penalties and tax consequences.

There will be individual tax and financial consequences when considering special assets such as long-term investment plans, vacation properties, properties or businesses attached to you or your spouse, partnerships, investment properties or second homes, timeshares, and your home. It depends on whether you decide to share or liquidate your interests at the time of the dissolution of your marriage. These items should be considered carefully with a professional advisor as they may represent large investments or a great portion of your accumulated wealth. Your attorney can support you in these areas as they will have access to resources such as well-trusted banking advisors, title companies, real estate attorneys, realtors, business bankers, investment officers, and other professionals within their realm of expertise.

When considering a dissolution of marriage, a best practice regarding accounts, investments, and credit is establishing your own as soon as possible. Open your checking, savings, money market, CD, retirement investments, credit cards, and other credit accounts. Begin your financial relationships if possible. Do not be in a hurry to move or close long-term relationships with banks or other financial institutions, as this may have tax or credit consequences.

You must prepare to move on with your life without dependency on another spouse or exposing your credit. You need to prepare to become self-sufficient. If you are not currently working outside the home, consider how you will generate sufficient income to move on while maintaining your current lifestyle.

If you have minor children or other dependents, let's think about how they will maintain their current standard of living. Your income? Spouse's income? Child support? Living assistance? Alimony? It's your future and that of your dependents. Separate your feelings from your decision-making at this vulnerable time by relying on your attorney or their support network for professional advice.

Leave the decision or at least advise phase to professionals who can counsel you without sentimental involvement. Your and your family's financial future may be at stake. It is time to separate emotions from good decision-making, and this is where your attorney and their network of experts come in to help as trusted advisors on your future finances. Careful planning and seeking professional financial and legal advice will lower your stress throughout the dissolution process.

When planning for dissolution of marriage, make sure you have your credit, separate and individual from your spouse, and close or limit any credit facility where the present credit facility is available for use by your spouse. Do not rely on short-term cash flow from joint credit cards or other joint credit facilities, as your spouse can cancel or limit the available joint credit facility. Best practices suggest you should not rely on short-term credit to solve your short-term cash flow needs. If you use short-term credit as a solution for cash flow, begin making repayment plans immediately.

Your credit score is very important, and taking care of your credit can affect future purchases such as real estate, car loans, consumer loans, personal loans, and credit cards. Guard your credit rating, as credit may be limited or unavailable to you with a low credit rating. Credit ratings affect the amount of future credit you may have, interest rates that you may pay, rental rates, and even the jobs or careers you may want. There are ways to improve your credit rating, but they all involve time.

Another topic for this section would be the level of trust you may have in your spouse now. You may be the best of friends, but I dare to say, trust only fiduciary relationships or your attorney. It is sad to say, but most individuals are looking out for themselves and their future during this time.

No matter how close the relationship may have been, the best practice is to review your credit report, bank statements, property titles, deeds, vehicle titles, and any other long-term assets monthly. In contrast, the dissolution has not yet been completed. Establish your credit and assets as soon as possible. There have been many cases in which, unfortunately, the person you believe you know will act in their self-interest to obtain the upper hand in negotiations.

The people you may have trusted the most, your partner, your friend, your confidant, may be questionable and not quite the people we thought we knew. Think about what got you to this point. They certainly look and act like trustworthy individuals, or they did at one point. Protect yourself financially. Trust the people who represent you to advise you, as they have likely seen many scenarios that, unfortunately, have left them questioning the true nature of people. Many times, this side of folks only shows itself under stressful conditions.

If everything turns out as well as it seems, fantastic! Expect the worst, protect yourself, and be happily surprised when everything goes well! Possession may not be 99% of the law (only your attorney can tell you this), but it certainly goes a long way in your financial negotiations. The best practice may be to secure accounts, real estate, and other investments as soon as your attorney can recommend. This is the time to heed their professional advice.

Planning is the key to financial success. I hope this discussion has been helpful to you and will help ease the dissolution process and provide subjects to consider as you travel through your financial journey. We wish you much success.

Chapter Nine
Divorce and Credit

By: Chris Colston

Do you want to be taken seriously? Then take things seriously.

Money talk, or more so, non-money talk, can destroy a marriage. This includes things like hiding money, hiding debt, overspending, underspending, and also financial abuse. Marriage is already hard because you are walking into unknown waters. No one teaches us what we need to do or know about money. No one teaches us about credit or finances. Often, our money mentors and parents are not real mentors because they had no one to teach them, and they are ashamed of their mistakes.

How often do we take our advice? How often do we go by our gut feelings?

What should you be doing if you believe you are walking down the path to a divorce?

Step #1: Saving

Get aggressive with your savings. Set a four-month target. Your vision is your mission. An apartment complex will require at least three months of rent to move in: The first month, the last month, and a month for a security deposit. Are you ready for this? If you don't have this amount, moving out of the marital home and into your own place will be very difficult.

Most people spend most of their time on defense, playing the cards they received instead of moving to a different table with different cards. Get aggressive and make this happen.

Step #2: Not Spending

How can you save if you are overspending?

It doesn't matter how much money you make monthly or yearly. What matters is how much of that money you are keeping in savings.

- To keep track of your spending, go to www.Mint.com.

- Separate your wants from needs.

- Avoid using credit cards to pay bills, even if you're getting points!

- Cut your crap memberships: Gym, cable, live stream, XM Radio, nails, hair, golf, Instacart, Hulu, Netflix, Amazon Prime, Disney Plus.

- LOOK AT THE FINANCIAL AFFIDAVIT.

Amplify your strength!!!

Step #3: Understand and Eliminate Joint Debt

DEBT will always be the killer of dreams. The more debt you have, the more money you give to the creditors, which tend to be BIG banks.

When you have joint debt, two people owe the debt. You cannot get out of that debt unless one of the two individuals pays it off or is refinanced by one debtor or the other. Joint debt can include credit cards, store cards, student loans, mortgages, lines of credit, automobile loans, and personal loans. Make sure you are aware of all joint debt in your marriage so you can be prepared to deal with any debt that has been racked up while you were married.

When preparing for a divorce, you must minimize and pay off as much joint marital debt as possible. This will leave you with less debt to divide between you and your spouse. Less debt means less of your after-divorce income goes towards debt.

Step #4: Gather Joint Assets

An asset is anything of value that has been obtained during the marriage. Some assets are obvious, like the home you live in or the cars you drive. Other assets, like a jet ski, boat, and retirement accounts, are not as obvious. It's important to gather as much information on all of the assets in your marriage so you can better understand where you stand financially. You should also get the original titles of any assets you own.

Step #5: Determine What You Are Willing to Lose

Discipline equals freedom, and sometimes that means cutting ties. Are you willing to lose those luxuries that you are accustomed to? You will no longer have financial help to pay for those luxuries! Remember, they are only luxuries, not necessities. Now may be a great time to trade in your car and get a cheaper car to save money quickly. This could be a car with a lower payment or which consumes less gas. You could save on the car payment, insurance, and gas, which is a big plus when trying to reduce expenses.

Step #6: Gaining Financial Independence

When a divorce is coming down the road, you have to start establishing some financial independence.

Start by opening a checking account in your name at a different bank from what your partner has. If you have concerns about your spouse opening your mail, open up a P.O. Box with a physical address instead of a P.O. Box address. Use this address for your new checking account.

This will allow you to be ready to start using your account instead of a joint account when the divorce is filed.

Make sure that you check your credit. If you have any outstanding issues with your credit, start working on a resolution immediately. This will allow you to start positioning yourself to get approved for a new home after the divorce is filed. Landlords frequently check potential tenants' credit for rental approval.

Track your spending using the tools at mint.com or any similar program. Start paying attention to your and your family's spending. This will prepare you for negotiations on obtaining or paying support.

The knowledge you will get from financial independence is priceless. You will know where every dollar goes and how it gets assigned to things. You can put a name on each dollar, not your partner's. You will stand on your own two feet.

The cons of being financially independent are that you no longer have the safety blanket or your spouse. You also cannot blame another person for being broke. Extreme measures are now being taken, and you must own up to them.

It is far better for a man to go wrong in freedom than right within chains. Don't chase perfection. Get started. It will all soon align.

Step #7: Are Your Finances Ready? Make Plans!

Do everything you can to follow steps #1 through #6. If you are not getting the momentum and results you wanted by month four, humble yourself and ask for help. Your friends and family want to see you happy.

If, for any reason, you cannot finance the car by yourself, see if a family member can do short-term, joint financing with you. Short-term financing means that, after 6 to 12 months, you will refinance the car in your name and take them off the loan. This could also mean you trade in the car and get another car in your own name. This is not the time to get an expensive car. You will burden your credit and your co-signer's credit, so save the nice car until you can afford it. If you need this help, do not lease a car. Breaking or refinancing a lease is much more difficult than refinancing or trading in a financed car.

Pro Tip #1

Need a quick boost on your credit? You can be added as an authorized user to a family member's or friend's credit card. This will help your credit history, usage, and overall credit performance. You should only do this with a trusted friend or family member who is a wise money manager.

You only want to be added as an **<u>authorized user</u>**. Do not co-sign on any new credit cards. Being an authorized user will not affect their credit, but it can significantly help yours. In six to 12 months, once you are more stable and your credit is better, you can remove yourself from their credit card. This is a short-term fix to achieve that six-month goal of being prepared before the divorce.

My Story

In my divorce case, the most difficult times were during the divorce. The emotional rollercoaster, the doubts, and the pain were difficult, but also the chess match and the poker match that comes with it. Everyone is trying to get the divorce done and finalized, but it is never that easy. Remember when you got married? That was the day you invited the government into your financial affairs. Now they want you to take care of those you love and left behind. The financial paperwork has to be done soon after the divorce is filed. Talk about pressure!

I have two young kids. My daughter was six, and my son was nine at the time of the divorce. I had to go and find a place to live near my office and not too far from the kids' house. I had the largest office in the building, which was fully staffed, and I had creditors breathing on my neck and back. During the marriage, we incurred debt. Some of the debt was dumb debt, some was mismanagement of money, and some was emergency debt, but if you caught the pattern, DEBT is DEBT.

At the time, I did not know what to do or how to endure all this pain. This was when I reached out to my therapist. Although I added more pain to my case, I knew I had to fix my past mistakes. The only way to save the present and set myself up for the future was to ensure I was fixing my mistakes. With my attorney, accountant, and therapist, a plan was set to ensure I walked away from my divorce in the best way possible. This was a difficult goal, but in the end, we achieved it.

I downsized my office space. I moved into the smallest office in my building. I'm so fortunate that my realtor and landlord are such great people. They helped me out so much. I'm forever grateful to them. I had to downsize my staff. This was a hard thing to do, but I couldn't keep them wondering what would happen to the business, me, and their families. I started communicating better with my ex. We had to do what was best for our children and us. Empathy isn't good for life; it's good for business.

It is never about how much money you make. It is about how much money you keep per month. My company represents many wealthy individuals, including musicians, actors, athletes, attorneys, and doctors. We review their financial and credit profiles, and many do not have six months of reserves in savings. You need to cut the fat off your expenses, and I did that. I stopped going to my favorite restaurant, I stopped buying these expensive drinks, I stopped shopping for these expensive clothes, and I started living a much simpler life. My dear friends are still my dear friends. My acquaintances are still my acquaintances. I had to survive, and I survived. Thank God for ramen noodles, chicken wings, and macaroni salad.

Pro Tip #2

Please keep track of the financial responsibilities that you have with your ex! DON'T SEND CASH. Every dollar you send should be sent with a check or money app. This will allow you to keep track of all payments and allow you to add a reason for that payment. You should print and keep each month's transactions in a binder. This will give you peace of mind AND help your accountant and divorce attorney during your case. Plus, it sends the message to your ex that you are on top of your finances and that curveballs will not be allowed.

Divorce Process

During the divorce process, people get themselves into a large financial mess. They are now trying to show and prove to their ex that they made a mistake. They are trying to prove to themselves that they are worthy. They are trying to heal wounds from the past by wasting money and often getting into debt. Please do not buy yourself a new and more expensive car. Do not rent that penthouse at your city's new and most hip building. Do not go on a shopping spree. This is the time to simplify your life, live below your means, and spend quality time with your children, family, and dear friends. This will allow you to heal yourself from traumas and this huge divorce blow. Be as calm and logical as you can be under pressure.

Discipline will always equal freedom. After the divorce is finalized is the time to put yourself back together and become stronger and better than ever. The only way to do this is to not make the same mistakes you made before. This includes all of the financial mistakes of your past.

If your credit took a hit due to the divorce, it is time to start fixing it. Please hire a professional to do this. It can take a lot of time to fix the problems you caused, but they can be fixed. A good credit repair company should explain your credit's pros and cons.

What credit cards do you have that are in good standing? What negative credit cards do you have? These might be the ones you missed multiple payments on or stopped paying because you couldn't afford them during the divorce. If you have student loans, are you repaying them on time? Will you refinance your car to remove that family member who helped you out, or will you refinance it to lower the interest rate? Do you have to refinance the house to remove your ex from the mortgage? Do you need to buy a house within the next few years? It's important to know what your financial moves need to be to ensure that you are moving toward success.

To move forward with your financial goals, you need patience, a game plan, and someone to guide you and hold you accountable. This is when you need to be tough because it will get hard, but you will achieve your goals.

Make sure that you continue to monitor your credit online. The best website or app for this is Experian.com. It will give you a full monthly breakdown of your credit scores, credit card spending, monthly payments, credit inquiries or who is checking your credit, addresses you have used in the past, and different variations of your name. If there are incorrect addresses in your credit report, it may be a red flag of identity theft. This is the same concern if there are name variations you do not recognize. The Experian website and app will be of great value to you in keeping track of your credit for a nominal amount.

Your money financial app should be Mint.com. This website and app will help you keep all your finances in one hub. You can add your personal checking account, savings account, business checking account, credit cards, loans (personal or school loans), automobile loan, mortgages, and investments. You can check daily to see how much money is coming in, how much you are spending, and where you are spending it. You can also see the interest rates you are paying on credit cards, the interest you are paying on your automobile loan, how much interest you are paying on your mortgage, and how your investments are doing. Knowledge is power.

Money comes and goes, and you want to enjoy the fruits of your labor, but you have to be very careful not to waste the fruits of your labor because your goals will become more distant. Perfectionism leads to procrastination, which leads to paralysis. Your game plan does not need to be perfect. The outcomes do not need to be perfect. You need to start.

Chapter Ten

Personal Injury and Family Law: How the Two Are Connected and What You Should Know

By: Janelle Vega, Esq.

Introduction

Have you ever wondered what would happen if you got into an accident during your divorce? Are you allowed to claim your injuries without your spouse knowing? What if you wait to settle your injury case until the divorce is finalized? Will your spouse get half of your settlement money? Can you put the settlement money into a separate bank account and not say anything? The honest answer to the above questions is that it depends.

Many factors go into answering the above concerns, and it also depends on where in Florida the personal injury case is being handled. These are all valid questions that can come up if you are injured due to an accident and want to pursue a personal injury case.

In this chapter, we will delve into the different types of issues that can arise related to personal injury settlements and insurance when individuals are going through a divorce, will go through a divorce, or have already gone through a divorce. A divorce can be a stressful event in and of itself, and there are a lot of other aspects of daily life, such as dealing with a car accident case, that can be affected by the split.

Statutes of Limitations

Under Florida law, the general rule is that individuals have four years from the accident date to bring a claim for their injuries against the at-fault individual or company. This applies to automobile accidents, trucking accidents, motorcycle accidents, trip-and-falls, slip-and-falls, dog bite cases, and almost any other accident you can think of. This is called the statute of limitations. Individuals wishing to bring a personal injury case must file a lawsuit within four years to preserve their rights. Once the lawsuit is filed, the statute of limitations no longer applies. Of course, there are always exceptions and nuances to the general rule.

For example, for medical malpractice cases, individuals who believe they have a malpractice claim generally have two years from the date of the malpractice to bring a claim for negligence against the medical provider. The exception to the rule is that individuals have two years from when they knew or should have known the malpractice occurred. The classic example is when a person goes into surgery, and the surgeon leaves a foreign object in their body, which is not discovered until three years after the surgery. This would fall under the exception since it happened two years after the accident but was not discovered until three years after the surgery.

In addition, another area included in personal injury cases is worker's compensation cases. Although these are also considered accident cases, different rules apply concerning the statute of limitations for worker's compensation cases. Individuals injured at work have the right to bring a worker's compensation case irrespective of fault.

If you file a worker's compensation case, you can also file a personal injury case against a negligent third party. However, you have one year from filing your worker's compensation case to file a lawsuit against the negligent third party. Not all companies are required to carry worker's compensation insurance, so it is important to speak to an attorney so they can review your case individually to make sure you preserve your rights.

Frequently Asked Questions

Now that we have discussed the general rules concerning deadlines for bringing a claim for your injury case, let's get into some of the frequently asked questions mentioned above.

I got into an accident recently, and I am contemplating getting a divorce now. What should I do, and how will the divorce affect my case?

First, remember your statute of limitations in Florida for accidents to preserve your right to bring your case. Next, you have different options if you were injured and are now contemplating a divorce. First, you must determine whether you were injured due to the accident. Sometimes people have accidents that do not result in any injury. If that is true for you, there is no personal injury case.

You should know that, in Florida, if you are involved in an accident and are injured, your legal spouse has the right to bring a "loss of consortium" claim. A loss of consortium claim is a claim brought by your spouse alleging they have suffered a loss of your comfort, society, love, affection, companionship, and care, as well as loss of intimacy due to the accident. Your spouse has the right to bring this independent claim. The claim has value and is recognized under Florida law.

Suppose you have been injured and you have completed all medical treatment associated with the accident. In that case, your first option is to hire a personal injury attorney to send a pre-suit demand to the insurance company for your injuries. A pre-suit demand is a letter that your attorney sends to the insurance company that includes a narrative of your injuries, treatment, past medical expenses, and future cost of treatment for your injuries. It is an attempt to settle your case with the insurance company before filing a lawsuit. If you choose this route and your case is settled, the insurance company will send you a release to sign. The insurance company will always ask if you are legally married because they want to include your spouse on the release since they have the right to bring a claim for the loss of consortium, as mentioned above.

What happens if your spouse does not sign the release?

This can be problematic and could cause the settlement to fall through. If your spouse is being difficult about signing the release, consider offering them a portion of the settlement funds or having your attorney advocate to the insurance company to include monies for their loss of consortium. Your spouse could also hire their attorney to advocate for their loss of consortium. However, having two separate attorneys to represent a single couple never looks good since it makes it seem as if the marriage is rocky. If the marriage is rocky, it would be hard to believe that the non-injured spouse truly has a claim for losing consortium. Remember, the value of the loss of consortium claim is usually nominal compared to the value of the claim of the injured party, which is another reason why a personal injury attorney would likely not take on this independent claim alone.

Your attorney will proceed with litigation if you cannot settle the case with a pre-suit demand. Litigation means your attorney will file a lawsuit in court on your behalf for your injuries. Once again, you have the option of including your spouse, but if you are contemplating a divorce, then it is likely the loss of consortium claim is questionable. One reason that lawyers include spouses in lawsuits is to extend the attorney-client privilege to the spouse. That way, the defense attorney is not privy to any conversations had between the couple and the attorney regarding the accident. Suppose the spouse is not included in the lawsuit. In that case, technically, the defense attorney is allowed to ask about any conversations the spouse has had about the accident with the attorney regarding how the accident happened, injuries, treatment, etc.

If the spouse is named a party in the litigation, they are permitted to sit in on the deposition of the injured party. This is key for building a credible and successful case. Once the case settles, the release will again include a space for your spouse to sign off. In litigation, your spouse will have been offered an amount for the loss of consortium and will be able to walk away with that in hand.

What if I do not want to include my spouse in the case?

If you do not want to include your spouse in the case due to the possibility of divorce, you also have a few options. Sometimes spouses have no interest in being involved anyway, so this might be an option for you. Otherwise, you can always wait until the divorce is finalized before bringing your claim. Make sure that if you choose this option, you have been treated by a medical provider for your injuries immediately after the accident and finalized your treatment. Each case is different; you may have a quick and amicable divorce. Otherwise, consider the general four-year statute of limitations to bring your claim.

Sometimes, individuals hire an attorney and bring a personal injury claim without notifying their spouse. The consequences of doing this vary by jurisdiction. There have been cases where the spouse is later made aware of the settlement and, during the divorce proceedings, argues that the settlement funds are marital property and are entitled to half of the monies. I will go into a more detailed explanation of this scenario below.

Will my injury settlement be affected if I owe child support?

Yes. Under Florida law, if you are in arrears on child support payments and have a personal injury case that settles, a lien can be placed on the settlement proceeds to ensure payment of the child support owed.[2] Your spouse who is owed child support can notify your attorney of the outstanding child support owed. Your

---

[2] See Dept. of Revenue OBO Karen Springer v. Peter Springer 800 So. 2d 700 (Fla. 5th DCA 2001) (holding that imposition of a lien against the prospective proceeds of father's workers' compensation settlement, for purposes of satisfying his child support arrearage, was appropriate mechanism to protect proceeds from improper diversion).

attorney must notify the Department of Revenue and/or the Child Support Enforcement agency. In addition, the insurance company paying out the settlement proceeds should also be placed on notice. Sometimes the attorney can negotiate a deal on the amount of child support owed, but it depends and is on a case-by-case basis.

Does my injury settlement count as income for child support or taxes?

In Florida, personal injury settlement proceeds are not considered income to include it on your taxes. That is why your injury settlement, both pre-suit and post-litigation, is "tax-free".

However, regarding child support, at least one court in Florida has held that worker's compensation benefits are included as income when a court determines the amount of a parent's child support award.[3] Florida has a

---

[3] See Dept. of Revenue OBO Karen Springer v. Peter Springer 800 So. 2d 700 (Fla. 5th DCA 2001) (noting that because the worker's compensation law is not only to protect the worker but also to protect the worker's dependents, worker's compensation benefits are included as income when calculating child support).

strong interest in protecting children, and courts will look out for a minor's interest in all aspects, including financially.

Is the personal injury settlement considered marital property?

This question comes up a lot, and the answer is, of course, "It depends." It depends on what jurisdiction you are in. In Florida, there is a presumption that funds received during the marriage are marital assets. You can overcome the presumption by introducing evidence that the funds are nonmarital. Florida statutes also provide that nonmarital assets may include "[a]ssets acquired separately by either party by non-interspousal gift, bequest, devise, or descent, and assets acquired in exchange for such assets."

In a personal injury case, the presumption can be overcome by ensuring the release clearly states what portion of the settlement award is for lost wages, future loss of earning capacity, past medical bills, future medical bills, past pain and suffering and future pain and suffering.

In classifying personal injury awards acquired during the marriage, Florida follows the "analytical approach."[4] The analytical approach considers the purpose of the portions of the personal injury award when classifying them as marital or nonmarital. Under the analytical approach, the marital property subject to distribution includes the award amount for lost wages or lost earning capacity during the parties' marriage and medical expenses paid out of marital funds during the marriage.

The nonmarital property belonging to the injured spouse includes the portion of the damage award for pain and suffering. The Florida Supreme Court has further stated that if there are any personal injury funds for which no allocation can be made, the funds should be classified as marital.[5] Thus, following the Florida Supreme Court's holding, if the release or settlement agreement in your injury case does not allocate the settlement proceeds to any specific category, the entire settlement can be classified as marital funds. This means when

---

[4] See Roth v. Roth, 312 So. 3d 1021 (Fla. 2nd DCA 2021).
[5] See Weisfeld v. Weisfeld, 545 So. 2d 1341 (Fla. 1989).

proceeding with a divorce, those funds would be subject to equitable distribution between you and your spouse, even if you were the one who suffered the injury. The fact alone that you were the one who suffered injury does not transform the settlement proceeds from marital to nonmarital.

In Miami, Florida, the Third District Court of Appeal is the appellate court for the Eleventh Judicial Circuit. The Third District Court of Appeal has previously held that a personal injury award was nonmarital property (thus, no need to split with a spouse).[6] Similarly, the Second District Court of Appeal has previously held that the injured parties' settlement qualified as a nonmarital asset upon receipt.[7] Further, another Florida court has held that when there is unrebutted evidence, such as testimony and language in a release that states the personal injury settlement is for future injuries, losses, and damages, the settlement is

---

[6] See Mazzorana v. Mazzorana, 703 So. 2d 1187 (Fla. 3d DCA 1997).
[7] See Valentine v. Van Sickle, 42 So. 3d 267 (Fla. 2nd DCA 2010).

considered separate property and a nonmarital asset.[8]

The bottom line, and the safest bet to ensure your injury settlement funds remain yours and are not subject to a split, is to have language in the release that the funds are for pain and suffering under the Florida Supreme Court's holding noted above.

Do I need to update my car insurance after a divorce? What policy should my children be on?

Suppose you are contemplating a divorce or have finalized a divorce and have children who are of driving age. In that case, you should review your auto insurance policy and make the necessary changes to cover all household members. Typically, when taking out an auto insurance policy, your agent will ask who else lives with you in the household. Always make sure to list all members of the household, especially those who have a license. If your

---

[8] White v. White, 705 So. 2d 123 (Fla. 2d DCA 1998).

children split their time between parents and the children drive, then each parent should have the children listed on their auto insurance policy.

Now, I know what you're thinking. This will cost me a fortune. Adding your teenage children to your auto insurance policy will raise your monthly premium. It is more expensive not to add them to your policy, get involved in an accident, and then have your insurance company deny coverage because you never told them they reside with you, even part-time.

This is a material misrepresentation, one of the strategies insurance companies use to deny coverage and insurance benefits. Remember that insurance companies, even your own that you've been with for years, are businesses. They are in the business of looking out for themselves and saving money. If your insurance company denies coverage, you could lose thousands of dollars of potential coverage for your child's medical treatment, thousands of dollars for your property damage, and thousands of dollars of potential coverage for their injuries.

You may think, "I'm not going to add my child to my insurance because even if they get into an accident, they have health insurance." While it is great that your child has health insurance, please remember that, under Florida law, the mandatory $10,000.00 of personal injury protection is primary insurance when someone is injured due to an automobile accident. Health insurance is secondary.

What does this mean for you? Suppose your auto insurance company denies coverage due to a material misrepresentation. In that case, your child will not have the first $10,000.00 of personal injury protection (PIP) benefits to pay their medical bills. They can use their health insurance. However, when it is time to claim the at-fault driver, the at-fault driver's insurance company will have a "PIP set-off" since PIP is required for all drivers under Florida law. This means that the at-fault auto insurance company will essentially discount $10,000.00 from any potential award they offer your child for their injuries. No one wants this to happen, and of course, no one thinks it will happen to them until it does.

As noted above, the consequences of not including your children on your auto insurance policy (if they reside with you even part-time) far outweigh any potential cost-saving benefits. I highly recommend that you discuss this issue with your spouse if you are contemplating divorce. Suppose you are in the process of divorce or have recently been divorced. In that case, you should immediately review your auto insurance policy to ensure all household members are listed.

Also, update your new address with your auto insurance company if you move due to the divorce. Suppose you live at an address that is different from what is listed on your auto insurance policy. In that case, your auto insurance company can deny coverage since you did not update them with your new address. Some people intentionally do not update their insurance company with their new address, fearing their premiums will increase. As noted above, the consequences of not keeping your insurance company up to date are far worse than the amount of money you might save by doing so.

Conclusion

Divorce can be complex, but it does not always have to be. Concerning accidents, we never know when they will happen. The truth is accidents are part of life, and they happen when we least expect them. Hopefully, this chapter has provided insight to help you be better prepared if and when you suffer an accident.

If you have been involved in any accident and want more information on your rights, please contact me at Solorzano Law, (305) 363-1300. We represent accident victims throughout the entire state of Florida and the District of Columbia.

Here's How We Can Help You

By: Vanessa Vasquez de Lara, Esq.

CONGRATULATIONS!

You are now a much more prepared Divorcing Dad. In fact, you're probably more prepared than 90% of the clients that walk into our firm.

But I'm sure that you still have many questions about *your* specific situation.

We can help with that.

Our firm offers a free case evaluation to make sure that we can help with your unique legal circumstances. After the free case evaluation, we will schedule you for a consultation where you will speak with someone from our legal team that will explain how our firm can help with your legal case or, if we can't, point you in the right direction.

Your Next Steps

Now that your family problem has become a legal problem, after your initial consultation and making sure we're a good fit, you will have the opportunity to hire our firm.

When you hire us, we will review your goals and priorities for the case so we can prepare you for what's coming. We will also go over the details of your case so we can have a better handle on exactly what we're going to seek from the court. This will include the major categories of the children, division of assets and debts, and spousal support.

Within those topics concerning children, we're going to talk about parental responsibility (the ability to make major decisions for your children) and a time-sharing schedule (the number of overnights that the children will be spending with you and how many with your ex).

Next, we will discuss the division of assets, liabilities and debts. We will talk about what has been accumulated during your marriage, whether it's a house, retirement accounts, savings accounts, or brokerage accounts, and what debt has been accumulated, such as credit cards, mortgages, student loans, etc.

Lastly, we will cover "spousal support" (alimony). We'll discuss the length of the marriage and the difference in the incomes of both sides, as spousal support is largely determined by how much one spouse can pay and how much the other spouse will need.

If your case is an Uncontested Divorce, it means we will be trying to resolve it with your ex before court. We love helping divorcing dads settle their cases by making reasonable offers to their exes. This approach ensures you're saving your hard-earned dollars for your kids' college (instead of contributing to mine). When both sides are willing to be reasonable, this is the most stress-free and simple method of resolving your divorce.

But realistically, an Uncontested Divorce is not always possible. When your ex is trying to withhold your kids, or take you to the cleaners, or make false domestic violence accusations against you, we have to proceed with a Contested Divorce. This means we will need to file your divorce in court, and we may need a judge to make certain decisions to protect your rights. At that point, my team and I will be fighting for you to make sure you get what you deserve - time with your kids and your fair share of the assets.

My Encouragement to You

In truth, I wish I didn't have this job. I wish everyone could work it out and find a way to be happy together. If that's possible, I would encourage you to still try and do so.

But if it's not possible, I recommend that you walk into this process with your eyes wide open. This will be one of the hardest things you will ever do.

The reality is that divorce is literally something passing away. It's the death of your relationship with this person. It's the death of the future you envisioned for yourself, this person, and your children. It is the end of life as you have known it.

It's normal to grieve, much like you would grieve the passing of a cherished loved one.

Most people start a divorce while they're in this grieving period. They don't know what to ask. They don't know how to move forward. Having someone that you can trust, who's going to have your back, who's going to be on your team to help you through that process and help you through to get to the other side of that journey is important.

Because a divorce isn't just a death, it's also a birth. The beginning of a new life and your new reality.

My Hope for You

I hope after reading this book, you feel empowered. I hope you feel like a big group of expert friends sat down with you and explained the things you need to be thinking about as you're going through the divorce process.

I hope you realize you don't have to just act on assumptions or whatever you can find on Google. You have a team on your side who is here to help you get through one of the most difficult things you'll ever go through.

How to Get in Touch

If you would like to have your case evaluated, you can go to:

DivorcingDadsGuidetoCourt.com

There, you can schedule a free case evaluation where we can let you know if we can help you. If we can, we'll schedule a consultation with a member of our team who will give you the concrete steps to get your divorce started.

Resources

Thank you to all the professionals who shared their wisdom in creating this book.

- ❖ Dr. Gisell Lopez, PysD
- ❖ Rebecca Amster Cantor, Esq., LMFT
- ❖ Lee Heyward
- ❖ Dr. Aixa Goodrich
- ❖ Carlos Gutierrez
- ❖ Alina Nuñez, Esq.
- ❖ Liliana Delara
- ❖ Fidel Fernandez
- ❖ Chris Colston
- ❖ Janelle Vega, Esq.

Name: Dr. Gisell Lopez, PsyD

Title: Licensed Clinical Psychologist and Life Coach
Time practicing specialty: 17 years

Contact info:
Dr. Lopez Is In and Associates
786-471-6980 IG and FB @drlopezisin
DrLopezIsIn.com

Name: Rebecca Amster Cantor, Esq., LMFT

Title: Attorney and Psychologist
Time practicing specialty: 20+ years.

Contact info:
rebecca@amsterfamilylaw.com
305-670-5074
amsterfamilylaw.com

Name: Lee Heyward

Title: Founder of The Prosperous Image
Time practicing your specialty: 15 years

Contact info:
Lee@prosperousimage.com
www.prosperousimage.com

Name: Dr. Aixa Goodrich

Title: Functional Medicine & Chiropractic
Physician
Time practicing specialty: 23 years

Contact info:
305-271-7447
www.southfloridachiropracticcenter.com
& www.draixagoodrich.com

Name: Carlos Gutierrez P.A.

Title: Real Estate Broker Associate and Expert
Witness
Time practicing your specialty: 20 years

Contact info:
305-710-9655
Carlos@GGMiamiRE.com
www.GGMiamiRE.com

Name: Alina F. Nuñez, Esq.

Title: Attorney
Time practicing specialty: 18 years of practice
in Real Estate and Title Insurance, Wills and
Estate Planning and Probate law.

Contact info:
305-962-5959
intake@nunezlawfl.com
7700 N. Kendall Drive, Suite 607
Miami, FL 33156
www.nunezlawfl.com

Name: Liliana Delara

Title: Investment Adviser Representative
Time practicing specialty: 30 years

Contact info:
5401 S Kirkman Rd, Ste 310
Orlando, FL 32819
7700 North Kendall Dr, Ste 607

Name: Fidel J. Fernandez

Title: Banker
Time practicing specialty: 41 years in Banking
(Personal Banking/Commercial Banking,
Lending, Cash Management, Investments,
Executive)

Contact info:
786-291-3989 Personal Cell
305-552-1515 Office
fidel.fernandez@firstbankfla.com

Name: Chris Colston

Title: DC Financial Services LLC Partner—
Credit Advisor
Time practicing specialty: 21 years

Contact info:
305-951-8381
DCFinServices.com

Name: Janelle Vega

Title: Attorney
Time practicing specialty: 6 years

Contact info:
Solorzano Law 305-363-1300
janelle@solorzanolegal.com
solorzanolawpllc.com

www.ingramcontent.com/pod-product-compliance
Lightning Source LLC
Chambersburg PA
CBHW061504050726
47593CB00002B/440